THE
MENTOR
MYTH

THE
MENTOR
MYTH

HOW TO TAKE
CONTROL OF YOUR
OWN SUCCESS

DEBBY CARREAU

bibliomotion
inc.

First published by Bibliomotion, Inc.
39 Harvard Street
Brookline, MA 02445
Tel: 617-934-2427
www.bibliomotion.com

Printed in the United States of America

Library of Congress Cataloging-in-Publication Data

Names: Carreau, Debby, author.
Title: The mentor myth : how to take control of your own success / Debby
     Carreau.
Description: Brookline, MA : Bibliomotion, Inc., 2016. | Includes
     bibliographical references and index.
Identifiers: LCCN 2015039237| ISBN 9781629561110 (hardcover : alk. paper) |
     ISBN 9781629561127 (ebook) | ISBN 9781629561134 (enhanced ebook)
Subjects: LCSH: Career development. | Vocational guidance. | Success in
     business.
Classification: LCC HF5381 .C343 2016 | DDC 650.1—dc23
LC record available at http://lccn.loc.gov/2015039237

To my family:
Todd, Josh and Jenna, you make it all possible

CONTENTS

INTRODUCTION

The Mentor Myth

Find a mentor: this is often the beginning and the end of advice for professionals looking to grow their career. I have worked in human resources for more than two decades, and never has there been such an emphasis on mentoring as there is now. In my view, *mentor* is among the most overused buzz-words in the workplace today.

What is a mentor? Typically, a mentor is an older, more experienced person who helps guide your professional future. Mentor relationships can either be formal, organized through a mentoring program in your company, or informal, established through connections you make on your own. When you need feedback on your career trajectory or big decisions like changing jobs, a mentor can be a real catalyst for career growth. Unless you are part of a structured mentoring program, there are no hard-and-fast rules for how often you need to see or interact with your mentor. You might exchange e-mails every six months or sit down for lunch weekly. There is not even a limit on the number of mentors you can have; you may have one mentor or many.

Recently, the idea of mentorship has been radically

expanded from the description I've just given. In my line of work, I constantly field questions about mentors, and I read article after article discussing the importance of mentorship. Mentors have come to be seen as one-stop guidance shops, capable of omniscient, career-defining advice and advancement. If you do an Internet search of the word "mentor," prepare to be overwhelmed by the amount of advice meant to help you find, snare, talk to, properly utilize, keep, or break up with a mentor.

In today's work environment, it is a given that everyone—especially those underrepresented in their industries—needs a high-level mentor. I would even say that a lack of formal mentorship is perceived to be a serious, career-inhibiting problem. This means that a significant part of the existing literature is devoted to finding and building relationships with mentors (how do you get a high-level executive or master in your field to agree to mentor you in the first place?). If you read these articles without knowing anything about what mentors are, you get a strange impression of what mentoring means. Take a look at lists like "10 Killer Questions to Make the Most of Your Mentoring Meeting"[1] and "12 Questions You Should Ask Your Mentor ASAP."[2] Sample questions proposed in these pieces range from "Am I being crazy?" (please don't ask your mentor this—save it for your friends or your mom) to "Anything FORM—their family, occupation, recreation, and motivation" (again, exercise caution—there is a fine line between being interested and pandering). Neither of these questions, however, falls within the scope of traditional mentoring. Mentors are available as resources to give you perspective on how to build your career. Questions about negotiating salaries or navigating a job search are perfect for mentors when you need an outside, experienced perspective.

The obsession with mentorship has gotten so out of hand that January has been declared "National Mentoring Month,"[3] and widespread institutional problems like a lack of diversity in the workplace are blamed on a lack of mentorship. While I agree that mentors can be important for women and minorities in industries where they are underrepresented, mentorship is not a silver bullet that will magically eradicate systemic inequities.

This overblown attitude toward mentoring is exasperating because, having coached tens of thousands of young professionals through their corporate journeys, never have I said, "The key to your fate is in someone else's hands." Don't misunderstand me: mentors are important. Their counsel and war stories can be invaluable. You want people with the right perspective to give you advice and make introductions. Mentors are just one piece of a much larger puzzle, however. Your mentor is one person offering one perspective, and her advice may or may not be wise counsel.

From my two decades working in human resources, I have found that mentors are overutilized and undertrained, and they underdeliver. For example, people commonly make the mistake of taking a mentor's advice as canon, but blindly following a mentor's advice can have negative, even disastrous, results. A famous cautionary tale comes from Sheryl Sandberg: when she was considering taking her career-defining job at Google, a mentor of hers urged her not to do it—the opportunity was too risky and ill-suited for her, according to the mentor. Sandberg had the same experience when she was offered the position of COO at Facebook, arguably an even more important career move.[4] Her mentor discouraged her from taking the job, advocating for a position with a more traditional company. Think of the loss both financially and professionally if she had followed her mentor's advice!

I experienced a similar situation in a formal mentoring program during my first high-level HR job. I was assigned a mentor who, at first, was quite useful. He helped me build perspective and hone my strategic operational skills. Over time, though, the relationship began to change. If I was reluctant to take his advice, I heard about it—and other people did, too. This was unhelpful and damaging to the reputation I had carefully crafted. Eventually, the relationship devolved.[5]

Unless your mentor undergoes formal training, there is no guarantee she knows anything about being helpful to you. Even if your mentor *has* attended a mentor training program, there is no guarantee that the training was adequate. Being a source of wisdom for a young person with a quickly evolving career is a tough task. Would you feel comfortable weighing in on another person's career-defining decision (for example, which job offer is best)? Remember, mentors are human, too. They can be biased, narrow-minded, jealous, and competitive. Any and all advice from external sources should be taken with a grain of salt. You have to consider your mentor's background, expertise, and motivations.

Additionally, many professionals enjoy mentoring but do not have the time to commit to a mentor–mentee relationship. An advisor who will look in on your career occasionally is different from a dedicated mentor who is consistently available as a sounding board. Many people do not take the time to establish their expectations as either a mentor or mentee, and thus end up disappointed. Another danger, especially if you are working in an industry affected by ongoing technological change, is that you and your peers might have a better understanding of the implications of new technologies than your mentors. The advice you receive from mentors, while well intentioned, may be outdated.

Perhaps the biggest risk of mentorship is that it gives people the impression that the outcome of their career is dependent on the actions and input of others. **The truth is: you are in control of your success.** Of course there are going to be factors outside your control—the economic climate, for example—but you dictate your own reaction to changing circumstances. This idea can be disconcerting: taking on the burden of success is a big responsibility. But if you are as driven as I am, you probably like the idea of being captain of your own fate. The good news is that you don't need to reinvent the wheel: in *The Mentor Myth*, I share solid strategies that will help you take control of your career. Instead of continually looking outward for career guidance, look inward: your own strengths, capabilities, and vision of success are all you need to succeed.

The advice and tools in this book aren't academic theories or made-up anecdotes; they rest on my twenty years of experience as a human resources expert. Following a successful career in corporate HR, I founded my own firm, Inspired HR, which I continue to run today. We support the human resources needs of hundreds of thousands of employees—we oversee hiring, performance and career development, terminations of staff, and everything in between. Witnessing the journeys of tens of thousands of professionals as they navigate goals that include climbing the corporate ladder and founding their own businesses has given me unique insight into the ingredients of professional success. While every person's journey is different, there are common themes that appear when you examine the journeys holistically. *The Mentor Myth* exposes those themes, offering my commentary on the career moves that lead to success and those that don't.

This is not the only book designed to help you think about your career. Plenty of guides give personal business advice, but they tend to divide into two categories: lifestyle balance (meditation, yoga, sleep) or high-level inspirational advice about "supercharging" your career. While these messages are empowering, readers often walk away with questions. On the surface, these two camps seem to promote conflicting demands on your time. Trying to do more yoga *and* be more committed to your career is admirable, but most people already feel like they are failing to optimize their busy schedules. Adding meditation *and* extra career counseling sessions pushes an already imbalanced schedule past the tipping point. Also, figuring out the mechanics of executing on more balance or more ambition is left up to the reader. Most people would probably agree that sleep is great, but they wonder *how* to fit more sleep into their frenetic lives. Similarly, many people would identify themselves as highly ambitious, and wonder what more "leaning in" translates to on an everyday basis. I have read all these books, but I rarely walk away with a clearer picture of *what* I need to be doing to advance my career. No one addresses the question of *how* to succeed.

This is what *The Mentor Myth* does—I will give you practical guidance for *how* to take ownership of your career. The purpose of the book is to provide you with the framework and strategies that will help you evaluate your goals, create a long-term plan to reach them, and be a top performer at work on the day-to-day. These are tested techniques that have worked for highly successful people at all levels in many industries. What skills do you need to develop to be valuable? What is your long-term game? Given the highly dynamic nature of the modern workplace, a career coach, manager, or mentor cannot determine this for you as effectively as you can. This book will give you the framework to drive your own strategy and be your own talent agent. By the time you have finished reading this book, you will have clear ideas about how to be your own agent, coach, or HR manager.

Chapter 1 begins with my career exploration tool, which will help you define your career goals—you can't reach a goal unless you know what it is. The tool will guide you through an analysis of your professional ambitions from six different perspectives (passion, economics, lifestyle, values, skill, and demand). You will be asked questions like: What does success mean to you? What is your end goal, professionally? Do your lifestyle expectations match the earning potential of your chosen career? The advice that follows in the rest of the book will be framed by your goals and will help you figure out how to achieve your dreams now that you've established them.

In chapter 2, we'll address your starting point. You will see transition throughout your career, with different jobs, different companies, perhaps different industries, and possibly even vastly different regions of the globe. No matter where you are in your career, the advice in this book will be relevant for you. There are, however, some special times of transition that require a little extra thought if you're going to optimize them. These are: when you are beginning your college education, when you are looking for your first job, when you are starting a company, and when you are looking to reenter the workforce after an extended absence. Chapter 2 discusses how to be strategic about planning your education and early career steps at these transition points.

Once you know what you want and where you are, we can get into the nuts and bolts of taking control of your career. Chapter 3 addresses how to manage your time effectively; none of the strategies in this book will help you unless you can make time to implement them. Then we'll move into establishing a personal brand (chapter 4), working on the "four Cs" (competence, confidence, communication, and commitment, in chapter 5), and establishing your network and sponsors (chapter 6). Chapter 6 is where you will find a more involved discussion of mentorship, but in the broader context of your network, sponsors, and peer groups. I will help you strategically incorporate external advice without being defined by it (remember, you are the one in control). Chapter 7 focuses on how to succeed at work by overpromising and overdelivering in everything you do. Chapter 8 discusses career transitions and taking risks to further your goals—no one has ever won by always playing it safe. Finally, we'll talk about the value of resilience—in other words, what to do when you fail (chapter 9).

After working through each chapter, you'll have a well-considered plan for taking control of your career. This is a comprehensive, easy-to-implement guide that requires only your brain, your time, and maybe a pen and paper (or your favorite form of digital note taking).

I have a habit of writing phrases that jump out at me on Post-It notes. My desks at work and at home are littered with neon squares scrawled with facts and phrases that grabbed my attention (my kids have even gotten in on this, and occasionally I'll notice a sweet note from one of them hidden in the display). One of my favorite notes, which I go back to over and over again, reads as follows: "It's boring to be average."

Is the phrase a little sappy and trite? Sure, but I truly believe in the sentiment. Whether I was working full time during university (because I liked the job), taking out a loan and buying into a restaurant when I was twenty-four years old, or taking the plunge and starting my own firm—all as I was getting married and raising kids—my journey has been anything but "average." To me, my way of life is normal—the key to pulling off my work success while juggling a full personal life (which, as a woman, I am asked about again and again) has been my conviction in my own abilities and my skill in thoughtfully creating and adjusting strategies. I also have the ability to pick up the pieces when I fail. While I have had many fabulous mentors and advisors during my journey, and I will always be grateful to them, my success is my own. Many times I bucked conventional advice and took a strategic risk that ended up paying off. If I hadn't stepped outside the expectations of mentors and friends and formed my own strategies, I would not have achieved the success I have today.

Fortunately, I don't have a monopoly on conviction, strategy, or bravery. These are character traits that you can deploy on your own, using this book as a guide. As you read, create your own plan to take control of your career and your life, and rise above the average.

CHAPTER 1

Taking Control of Your Career

What do you want to be when you grow up? Kids are fixated by this question, and, despite limited life experience, they usually have a clear answer. For example, my seven-year-old daughter wants to be a dolphin trainer by day and a doctor on the side. My son would like to be a sports announcer. That sounds more realistic than a dolphin trainer but I'm not counting on his career goal panning out, considering that he had a totally different answer last week—and a different one the week before that. We've run through everything from a cashier at A&W to president of the United States. But this constant evolution isn't a bad thing. In fact, adults could learn a thing or two from kids' focus on their future career—especially from the way their goals adapt based on their changing interests and on what they learn about the world.

Having a goal in mind becomes much more important as you begin to train and plan for your career. Most people spend more time working than they do with their spouse, kids, and friends, so your career shouldn't be an afterthought. I believe you can't be successful without an idea of where you are going; very few people accidentally find themselves CEO of a Fortune 500 company. Can you think of one corporate leader who attributes his success to just having showed up? Even tech company founders, who seem more focused on building cool stuff than building companies, had an idea that their product could catch on and worked obsessively toward its success.

Being a Fortune 500 CEO might not be your vision of success, but if you are reading this book, you are professionally ambitious. Ambition needs direction. Getting what you want in life, professionally and personally, requires *knowing* what you want. The earlier you can define that vision, the better. Granted, this vision might change over time. It could even change radically as you realign priorities. But before you lean in, you have to have an idea of what you are leaning *into*.

The tricky part is, I find that people don't put much effort into career planning. In my experience, they tend to let their next steps be defined by managers, or they just put their heads down and work really hard, hoping someone will notice them. When it comes to promotion, most of us are presented with a plan and then follow it. Ironically, research suggests this might have something to do with behavior learned in school—we are rewarded for following directions with good grades and positive attention.[1] We get points for getting everything right, not for taking risks or making mistakes. Very little about this operative strategy translates into getting ahead in your career.

To further complicate matters, millennials (the generation

born after 1982)[2] are expected to stay in jobs less than three years—meaning they will hold fifteen to twenty jobs during the course of their careers.[3] Even if you have a well-thought-out plan in place, how do you anticipate every one of those transitions? And if you don't do *any* planning, what happens to you? The chances of ending up in a profession you don't want to be in seem infinitely higher. Navigating a modern career seems to require the skill of a chess master, looking many moves ahead at any given time.

The conclusion here is that a successful career requires both planning and flexibility, two elements that at first glance seem diametrically opposed. But a closer look reveals that, in real life, the two are complements. You can't be expected to plot your exact career trajectory and later be totally comfortable when your dreams get blown up by a recession or the arrival of a child. What I am advocating is that you have an idea of where you are going and be willing to accept that your vision might change as life changes around you.

The good news is that better career planning is not dependent on input from other people, so you can set the mentor myth aside: you have control over whether you are thoughtful about your next career steps. You decide if you are going to have a long-term, strategic professional plan in place.

My intent is to help you think about the kind of life you want and how you will make that happen. Keep in mind that none of this advice is about finding that next rung on the corporate ladder. This chapter is meant to help you navigate the road map of your career with easy, practical steps; you need to define what success looks like and then align that vision of success with the career and lifestyle you would like to have.

The Career Exploration Tool

I wish I were able to go back and give my twenty-year-old self some practical career advice. While I ended up on a career trajectory I am proud of, I could have gotten there much earlier if I'd paid more attention to where I was going. After two decades in human resources, I have a much more nuanced perspective of what it takes to make a well-considered career plan.

When coaching people on their careers, I focus on six elements: passion, lifestyle, values, economics, skill, and demand. Thinking strategically about each of these elements lets you create a framework for a solid career map. And no matter where you are in your career (university, new grad, or seasoned veteran of the workforce), this tool is relevant. We can all make adjustments to either refine our vision, if we like where we are going, or radically change our plan, if we are unhappy. This tool helps you consider your professional journey from every angle, and it is worth revisiting often as you navigate your way to your professional goals.

Passion

In my HR consulting practice, I find that the average person spends 50 percent of her waking hours working, commuting, thinking about work, or returning texts, e-mails, and phone calls related to work. If you are a career-oriented person or a business owner, this percentage is probably even higher (and let's face it, some of us probably *never* entirely stop thinking about work). Chapter 3 will focus explicitly on time management, but the reality is that working takes up a majority of your time no matter how well you manage your day. If you spend all day disliking what you do, you will find it hard to motivate yourself to work hard enough to be successful.

In the last few years there has been some criticism of "following your passion," most notably by Cal Newport in his 2012 book *So Good They Can't Ignore You: Why Skills Trump Passion in the Quest for Work You Love*. The gist of this argument is that following a preexisting interest is not the best way to ensure you find your job satisfying. Instead, he says, you build passion as you become skilled at your job. It's human nature to like the things we're good at, so it is better to pursue careers within our natural abilities, whether or not we like them.

This is an interesting argument and probably mostly true. Every job will have disagreeable elements. However, having natural passion about *some* part of your career is pretty important. Even if you don't love your job, you have to like it. Research shows that happy workers are more productive workers.[4] You will be less likely to resent the time you spend at work and you will be more motivated to work hard if you are passionate about the mission of your job.

Following a preexisting interest (such as art, hockey, or skydiving) is also far more practical if you have a strategy in place for turning that interest into a monetizable career (there's a great book that incorporates this idea, *Finding Your Element* by educator Ken Robinson). If you want to be a writer, be realistic that this isn't initially (and may never be) a high-earning career. Have a clear plan in place for how you are going to support yourself while you are getting off the ground, as well as a backup plan for lean times.

The inverse of "don't follow your passion" is definitely true: don't do things you hate. I am sure there are people who are mercenary enough to suffer through high-earning jobs that are a daily misery—but I haven't met them. Every successful person I have worked with in my career has been energized by her job. It sounds trite, but when you like what you do, it often doesn't feel like work. Running my own business focused on creating great workplaces makes me excited to get going every day. That said, there are aspects of the business I don't enjoy: doing payroll and proofreading training materials are two of my least favorite tasks because, frankly, I'm not the best in the world at them. The solution: I hire people who do enjoy and excel at those two functions. The job gets done much better than I would have done it, and I don't have to suffer through it myself!

Also, note that your passion may not align with the salary you would like to earn (more on this in the next section). If that's the case, plenty of people find work they enjoy, and they follow their passion as a hobby. I know many successful businesspeople who are high earners and teach spin or other fitness classes for fun in their spare time. Plenty of other professionals I have come across blog, teach, or run side businesses that allow them to explore an interest that couldn't support them as a primary career.

Lifestyle

As you form your career goals, think about the kind of lifestyle you envision yourself having when you are older. This consideration has several elements, from your socioeconomic status to the level of flexibility you would like in your daily life. What kind of house would you like to live in? How many hours per week would you like to spend working? Are you willing to forgo free time for financial gain? Many professions that sounded appealing to you when you were ten or sixteen won't align with your vision of a successful life later on. Some of these careers are more whimsical—like being an exotic animal trainer or an astronaut—and a little maturity shows us that these are impractical lifestyles for most of us.

The concept of flexibility also applies to where you would like to live and how much you would like to travel. Jobs in sales generally require quite a bit of weekly travel, even at high levels. Banking or management positions at multinational corporations can mean moving around in order to get promotions. Are you willing to move or to spend a lot of time away from home in order to advance?

The key is to define what success means to you. In interviews I conducted with successful professionals at all levels, the idea that success has varying definitions was a common theme. Most of these people acknowledged that "life balance" was a tenuous concept. Having both a fulfilling personal and professional life is tough, and means making continuous trade-offs in order to keep it all going. If you can define at the outset your baseline level of success in each category, you can retain a little sanity.

This means asking yourself tough questions. Does success mean making lots of money? Does it mean a high-profile position? Does it mean getting to spend every summer with your children? Are you flexible on the hours you want to work, the location where you want to live, and the distance you want to commute? Your answers to these questions may change, but spend some time thinking about them now. It's a shame to put in years of work only to hit a glass ceiling when you realize you're not willing to move to Hong Kong to get that next promotion.

Weighing Professions

Maya was a talented, passionate ballet dancer with amazing stage presence, and she had a real shot at becoming a professional ballerina after she graduated from high school. Shortly before graduation, her mother sat her down and said, "Maya, you are a wonderful ballerina, and if you choose to pursue dancing professionally I will be behind you 100 percent, but I feel as though I need to make sure you have all the facts so you can make an informed decision." Her mother pulled out their family household budget to show Maya what it cost to support the family. Then she pulled out some salary research that showed what ballerinas earn and how many professional ballerina positions exist nationally. Maya changed her career trajectory, went to law school, and pursued ballet as a hobby. Today, Maya is a mother who works independently as a lawyer so she can dictate her own hours and spend time with her son.

Values

What you choose to do in life will also be influenced by your values. I can't give much advice about those—your values are your own—except to say that it is important to honor your personal values in your profession. There is no quicker way to resent your job than to fundamentally disagree with the mission and ethics of the company you work for.

To avoid professional contexts that would push you to compromise your values, you need to first identify what your values are and decide which are most important to you. Is it important that you work for a company that engages in fair trade, emphasizes environmental practices, or has a religious element? Perhaps you would like to be part of a company that has a strong emphasis on CSR (corporate social responsibility). Maybe you even want to work in a CSR-related function. Whatever the case, your values will inform your own personal mission and passion. The most successful job matches I have seen occur when a person's own mission overlaps with the mission of her company. Don't discount your values when evaluating a career path or employer. Take the time to research industries and companies to see how they fit with your beliefs.

Economics

The career path you choose can dramatically alter your earning potential. Even different functions or positions within the same company can have a material effect on your annual take-home pay. CEO-to-worker earning ratios (using salary data for the top three hundred and fifty revenue-producing U.S. companies, excluding Facebook—an outlier due to their high compensation—were 295.9-to-1 in 2013.[5]

Realize, too, that statistics on average earnings don't paint the whole picture. Certain careers are more secure than others. Management tracks with large, stable corporations in growing industries are generally a safe bet as long as you perform at work. Jobs that offer tenure or pensions, like certain teaching positions, are also quite stable. However, to state the obvious, in exchange for stability you usually trade earning potential. As the saying goes, the greater the risk, the greater the reward. Entrepreneurial endeavors or positions in sales may have turbulent earnings periods but could end up paying off in the long run.

I am not saying you must choose the career that offers the most money. You need to decide how important making money is to you and then be honest with yourself about whether your desired career can support the lifestyle you would like to have. If you'd like to be a cartoonist, don't count on being able to buy a million-dollar house in the first five years of your career.

If you are consciously choosing a lower-earning career path, educate yourself about managing your personal finances so that you can properly administer your assets and plan for life events like having a baby, sending kids to college, and retiring. In fact, such financial planning is a worthwhile exercise no matter how much money you earn. Plenty of resources exist to help you remedy any gaps in your knowledge (one of my favorites is a book titled *Well-Heeled: The Smart Girl's Guide to Getting Rich* by my good friend Lesley-Anne Scorgie).

Skill

The role your skill set will play in your career is straightforward: the better you are at what you do, the more successful you will be. Equally obvious, most skills can be improved. If you have a weakness in math or if you would like to be better at public speaking, take a class or seek out a coach. If you are not sure where your weaknesses lie, ask your manager where your skills could be stronger. An even more advanced tool to consider is a 360° feedback assessment that combines the perspectives of supervisors, peers, and your direct reports (if applicable).

Of course, it helps to choose a profession that is a good match for your natural talents. If you are excellent at interacting with people, think about a career in human resources, hospitality, or sales. Being naturally good at what you do is energizing and builds confidence, a trait that many people lack in their professional lives.

Keep in mind that no matter how hard you train, you may not be suited for some careers, based on your individual assets and skill set. No matter how many hours as I put in, I will never be a professional ballerina. However, I can use my professional skills to help the National Ballet School grow its business.

Demand

There's a reason we call it the "job market." As in any other market, supply and demand dictate how much employers are willing to pay you. Easy access to industry-specific employment statistics on the Internet means you can make an informed choice about the economics of your targeted career. Check out the U.S. Bureau of Labor Statistics' site (http://www.bls.gov/emp/ep_table_104.htm) to see which occupations are experiencing the highest levels of growth. Some careers that we assume will always be in demand are actually quite saturated (this has been true of the legal industry recently), so do your research before you choose a path.

FIGURE 1.1 Example of the career exploration tool.

CAREER EXPLORATION TOOL

Part 1: Weigh Career Elements

This exercise will help you explore the career elements that are most important to you. In the "weight" column of the table below please weigh the importance of each career element on a scale from 1 to 6, with **6** being the *most* important element to you in your career, and **1** being the *least* important to you.

Career Element	Statements to Evaluate	Weight (1-6)
PASSION	It is really important to me that I love my job.	
VALUES	The work I do must align with my personal values.	
ECONOMICS	Making a lot of money in my job is important to me.	
SKILL	I am willing to invest the requisite time and money to attain the skills I need for this career.	
DEMAND/ EMPLOYABILITY	It is really important to me that there be high demand for jobs in my field.	
LIFESTYLE (WORK–LIFE BALANCE)	I want a job that fits my lifestyle (has good work–life balance).	

Part 2: Evaluate Your Career Options

Now that you know the career elements that are most important to you, it is time to consider your career options. First, think about up to four career options you would like to pursue. In the following table, fill in each of your career options under the "Career Option" heading.

Got your possible career options? Great! Next, we will evaluate each career option against each career element. To do this, rank each possible career from 1 to 10 according to the six career elements, with **10** being the *highest possible score* for that career option, and **1** being the *lowest possible score* for that career option. For example: If I was deciding between being an investment banker, a lawyer, a doctor, and a teacher, I would start with the *passion* element and rank investment banker as a 1 (meaning I am not that passionate about it) and doctor as a 10 (I have always wanted to save lives). Complete this ranking procedure for each of the six career elements.

Career Element	Career Option 1: ( )	Career Option 2: ( )	Career Option 3: ( )	Career Option 4: ( )
PASSION				
VALUES				
ECONOMICS				
SKILL				
DEMAND/ EMPLOYABILITY				
LIFESTYLE (WORK–LIFE BALANCE)				

Part 3: Calculate Your Ideal Career!

You're almost there! Now that you have rated each of your potential career options according to the career elements, it is time to once again consider the weight of each element. To do this, take a look at the weights that you assigned to each career element above (the number from 1 to 6). Next, *multiply the ranking score (the number from 1 to 10)* for each career option, *by the weighting score (the number from 1 to 6)* for that career element. Place that number in the table below.

Last, *add* up all your scores for each column and write it in the "grand total" box. This will allow you to see what is the best career fit for you at this point. Note: the *higher* the score the *more* aligned the career option is with these important career elements, potentially indicating a more fitting and fulfilling career choice.

Career Element	Weighting (from part 1)	Career Option 1: ( )	Career Option 2: ( )	Career Option 3: ( )	Career Option 4: ( )
PASSION					
VALUES					
ECONOMICS					
SKILL					
DEMAND/ EMPLOYABILITY					
LIFESTYLE (WORK–LIFE BALANCE)					
GRAND TOTAL	X				

Online version available at www.mentormyth.com.

Still Feel Lost?

If you worked through the entire career exploration tool above and did not come to an answer, don't panic—this is not unusual. Sometimes we need time and experience to figure out what we want to do.

You can still be strategic about your next move. If you are still in school, the next chapter will help guide your choices. If you are in the workforce, pick a general industry or functional area that makes sense for you and then choose a job that will develop universally useful skills. Rotational programs at big corporations are designed to give you exposure to many different tracks without committing you to a specific one. Or maybe you would like exposure to different fields before you choose one. Management consulting and temp jobs are a great way to work across industries without being pigeonholed. Once you have a better idea of what you like, you can develop your expertise. Instead of worrying about finding the perfect career immediately and feeling paralyzed by indecision, experiment in a focused way that lets you take charge and design your life to meet your needs.

I will discuss this in more detail later, but an easy way to choose an initial path is to look at people you admire and emulate what they have done. Some of the most intelligent people I know say you don't have to be smart, you just have to know whom to copy (they call it "search and reapply"; find a strategy that works and then tailor it to your situation). Think about your role models and try to figure out why they appeal to you. Do you like their mission? Their lifestyle? The manner in which they manage? Sometimes the answer isn't obvious. Once you have the attraction pegged, take a closer look at your role models' professional journeys. Did they get an advanced degree, switch jobs every three years, or work abroad? Were there certain companies they worked for that they cited as especially invested in employee training or minority sponsorship? Clearly, every person's path will be different, but it's much easier to follow a proven path than to struggle through the weeds.

The Key to Great Planning: Expect Everything to Change

Having a vision for your career is invaluable, but you need to be able to make adjustments as you go. No matter how good you are at anticipating disruptions, you can never foresee all the factors that will cause you to reevaluate or tweak your vision. The key is to allow for change; your plans should be dynamic rather than fixed.

I have found that people are often too slow to make changes in their career. Either they are loyal to their company or simply get caught in professional inertia (change is hard work). The benefit of the career exploration tool is that it can serve as your framework for setting goals, tracking progress toward those goals, and reconsidering both your goals and your progress if you find them lacking. Set aside time every six months (or more frequently if you are inclined) to work through the career exploration tool as a way to measure whether your dreams match your reality. We tend to get so caught up in day-to-day events that years pass before we consider whether where we are headed is in line with where we wanted to go—or if our goals are even relevant anymore. Do not let your evaluations of your work life happen only in year-end reviews with your manager. You can and should take a big-picture look at your career progress with some frequency.

Apart from the changes you decide to make in your career trajectory, external factors can affect your career plans. One thing you should be aware of is the macroeconomic environment. If the economy is headed into a recession, what does that mean for you or your company? Is your industry undergoing a technological shift that will be important for you? Is there a greater demand for your specific skills in a different region of the country or the world?

Knowing the demand for your skill set is critical. It is also important to stay attuned to unforeseen career-boosting opportunities. Look both internally and externally for the kinds of opportunities that could take you to the next level. Often, these will be a bit risky or unconventional, so keep your eyes open. A piece of advice I've heard over and over is that it doesn't matter what company you are working for, it matters how fast that company is growing. A great example is Sheryl Sandberg's move to Google: while she had plenty of offers at more secure firms, taking a position at a start-up ended up being a highly strategic move that paid off.

In my late twenties, I underwent a major career change that was totally self-initiated. After being the managing partner in restaurants for seven or eight years, I knew the parts of the business I enjoyed (the people) and the parts I didn't like so much (working every night, weekend, and holiday). When it came to people, I loved not only interacting with the customers, I also loved the staff and was strong at building high-performing teams (this is the passion piece). My personal life was undergoing changes, too, and my values around having flexible time and being at home were shifting. I had recently gotten married and knew my husband and I would be starting a family. Working nights and weekends with an infant would be challenging, so I looked long and hard at my career trajectory and decided to move into a corporate HR role.

In theory, moving into the leadership team of the parent organization that owned the restaurants I worked for was a promotion. In reality, the change entailed a huge pay cut, considering I'd been working as a managing partner of a high-volume restaurant. I was all of twenty-five or twenty-six years old and had been earning a strong six-figure income for a few years. It was a real risk to sell my business interest and move to a position that started at $60,000 a year. Don't get me wrong, $60,000 was certainly a decent salary at the time, but it was only a fraction of my previous earnings. What would this drop in pay mean for my lifestyle? It was a scary proposition, considering that my husband and I were planning for kids, with all the financial commitment that brings.

But I knew what I wanted to do, I knew there was a demand for my skills, and I knew that if I took the pay cut, I could quickly close the earnings gap in the future. I reasoned that I could continue on a strong career trajectory as long as I invested in my technical education in parallel with my new job. I also knew if I delayed the decision, the opportunity might not exist five years down the road.

I took the job with the pay cut and never looked back. I closed the earnings gap in just eighteen months, and also got my professional designation in human resources. The financial success has been huge, but more importantly, I truly love my work in human resources to this day. I found an outlet for my entrepreneurial leanings by opening my own firm, Inspired HR, just after finishing my MBA. These were hardly changes I could have planned for, but making them required keeping my long-term goals in mind and moving aggressively when I needed to.

One thing you should absolutely do, so that you are prepared for either golden opportunities or layoffs, is keep your résumé updated. In this modern age, that means keeping your online profiles (like LinkedIn) updated as well. Check your various social media profiles and make sure they are up to date; the way you are branded online is a big factor in today's job market. Many people don't attend to their résumés and professional profiles because they worry it comes off as being disloyal. It isn't—it's just smart business.

Seven Tips for a Great Résumé

Think of your résumé as a marketing document for your personal brand. Reflect your personality in the formatting, but keep content professional.

1. In describing the work you've done, start with your areas of strength. List accomplishments with verbs, not as activities or tasks.

   Example 1: Opened seven new business units in two new markets.
   Example 2: Achieved highest GPA in the program.
   Example 3: Led the Student Council Corporate Social Responsibility Committee.

2. Include shortened web links so the interviewer can do further research easily. Examples include company links, social media, and any published articles or interviews that are relevant.

3. Always proofread carefully, and ask another person to review your résumé for you. Spelling and grammar mistakes are a no-no.

4. Get a professional e-mail address that you can include on the résumé. I can't tell you how many *sexyhotchick@gmail.com* e-mail handles I've seen. This line of thinking applies to your voicemail as well. I remember calling one CFO candidate and his voicemail greeting was Bruno Mars's "The Lazy Song." Needless to say, he wasn't the top candidate.

5. Instead of just dropping your résumé in an online bucket—where it will automatically go through the applicant tracking software and potentially get lost among the hundreds of other applications—always try to get a personal referral. A referral will put your résumé on top of the pile, increasing the chance that a human sees it before a computer screens it out.

6. Game the system: many companies use résumé parsers to weed through digital résumés, but you can outsmart the filters. Use the exact same language to describe your skills that is used in the job posting. That way, key words in your résumé will match what the computer program is looking for. Think of your résumé submission like a Google search; the more words that match the posting, the higher your résumé will rank.

Bonus tip: In addition to your résumé, submit a cover letter that is appropriate and relevant. Do your homework. Address the letter to the right person. Read the company's website, relevant new articles, and the company's annual report or press releases. In a sentence or two, tie in how your experience aligns with an area of focus for the company.

Extra-special bonus tip: Go for it! I find that men tend to be more aggressive than women when applying for jobs. Often, men will apply for positions even if they don't meet 100 percent of the qualifications—and they get the job. The lesson is that, to a certain extent, qualifications listed in a job posting are not always hard and fast. So if you see a position that you think you are right for and can make the business case for your candidacy, drop a résumé. You'll never get hired if you don't apply in the first place.

Putting It All Together

As you are working through your vision for your career, write down any thoughts—even half-formed ones—you might have about what you want to be on your résumé or the kinds of projects you want to work on. In one place, keep records of positions that seem interesting or companies that are doing cool work. If you are an entrepreneur, look at how your competitors are innovating. Did you come across a business profile of a successful businessperson in the *New York Times* that got you especially excited? Cut it out (or copy and paste) and compare it to the notes you have written down next to passion, lifestyle, and the other elements of the tool. By constantly evaluating your career goals and path, you will keep your road map fresh and relevant. Too many people end up hitting glass ceilings or working at jobs they don't like because they didn't take the time to plan where they were headed.

The fix is within your control. Know what success means to you. Be future oriented and thoughtful about your career goals. Adapt to changing circumstances without losing sight of what it is you really want.

CHAPTER 2

Laying the Right Foundation: Education and New Jobs

After completing the career exploration tool in the previous chapter, you should have a better sense of your professional goals. The rest of this book will give you the tools to start working toward those goals.

So where do you begin? No matter where you are in your professional journey, the advice in the following chapters will be useful for you. However, there are certain unique career "starting points" that are foundational and require extra planning. Designing your undergraduate education, starting your first job, starting a business, and reentering the workforce after an absence are all pivotal moments in your professional journey and will lay the foundation for what comes later.

If you find yourself at one of these critical points, this chapter is for you. It will help you frame the rest of the advice in this book, because your education and new job (or first job after an absence) are jumping-off points that everything else will build on. Even if you are not at one of these points, I recommend reading this chapter if you are interested in continuing your education (and everyone should be, in some form) or might someday take a leave from the workforce. As I said earlier, the key to success is great planning, and that includes planning your education and your sabbaticals. Schooling and work transitions are critical pieces of any career, and the advice in this chapter will help you create your own strategy.

Talking 'Bout That Education

Planning your career starts with your education, although not all people approach their schooling with this thought in mind. Many people go into postsecondary school following an interest or a passion without thinking about how marketable that degree will be after they have graduated. The same holds true for those of us who have pursued a graduate degree after time in the workforce.

I realize this sounds mercenary. After all, a degree—especially at a liberal arts institution—is meant to give you general skills that will make you effective in the workforce. I believe this is true, but I also believe it is important to envision *how* you are going to use these skills to earn an income down the line. What will your economics degree mean to you in ten years? How about your degree in philosophy?

The trouble is, when you are just beginning your higher education, you are young and have the endless possibilities of the world open to you—and you probably don't truly know what you want to do with your life. So how do you plan your education when you don't know what you're planning for? The answer is that it's complicated—there isn't really a right or wrong path when it comes to your schooling. And very few people follow a perfectly linear path through college and the early part of their career; usually, their journey involves a little exploring and testing things out.

I believe you should start with an educational focus in mind but be open to exploring other interests as they arise. You never know when you will hit on something you like, and you might cross things off the list that sounded nice in theory but weren't as great in real life (how many students enter school wanting to be a doctor and then very quickly change their minds?). At the same time, you always need to be thinking about how your area of study translates into a viable career that can support you financially. Remember, plans change. Research your options, know the demand for your major, and be okay with letting things evolve. The only real mistake you can make is doing zero critical thinking about where your education is taking you.

My own education was not a seamless, perfectly planned four years. I went to school with the idea that I was going to be a lawyer. Sounds like I had it all together, right? Wrong. The most popular TV show at the moment was a legal show with a female protagonist. My desire to be a lawyer had nothing to do with the kind of education or commitment it would take to get there (just a note, law is notorious for having lots of entry-level female lawyers who later leave to never practice again—what does that tell you about the lifestyle?).[1] I had no idea what a day in the life of an attorney looked like. I just thought it looked like fun! My first inkling that I had "chosen" a career that wasn't quite right for me was how I felt in the prerequisite classes for my degree. For example, instead of being engaged in the discussions in my philosophy classes, I was horribly bored. This seemed like a bad sign.

I wish I could say that I sat down and reevaluated my educational track with large sheets of data showing the current demand for each major coming out of my school. Or that I took an in-depth personality assessment that used my interests to prescribe professions. I did neither of those things. Instead, I started taking classes outside my discipline.

I got lucky because I soon hit on subjects that *did* interest me. I took an economics course that piqued my interest in business. I then took a sociology class that, as part of the course, covered fantastic business cases that focused on the human capital element of running a company. Fortunately, this was only my second year of college and I had time to point my studies in a direction different from the one I had originally planned. I was also working at a restaurant, which introduced me to the hospitality industry, an industry I truly enjoyed and joined full time, working nights and weekends while finishing school. I don't tell this story to illustrate how smart I was about choosing the right education for my career. If anything, the opposite was true; I explored different options and got lucky. But, I was always thinking about where my education would take me (and law ended up being an unattractive option). I believe many people have stories similar to mine. They started with an idea of what they wanted to do and ended somewhere different through a very nonlinear path.

With all these complexities in mind, how do you go about planning your education strategically? The first step is to look at the data. The reality is that the 2008–09 recession created a harsh climate for new graduates looking for full-time work. While the situation has improved in the last few years, it still isn't rosy. Unemployment rates for U.S. graduates ages twenty-two to twenty-seven fell to 5.6 percent in 2013[2]; however, more than half of employed new grads work at jobs that don't require a degree.[3] The old rule that a degree equals a job no longer applies. In addition to the lack of guarantee that your degree will supply you with a job, the cost of higher education has become onerous. Overall student debt in the United States stands at more than $1 trillion.[4] Paying back loans puts additional pressure on students to make sure that their degree is an investment that will produce returns.

I see two lines of thinking to mitigate the risk attached to your undergraduate or graduate degree. The first is both simple and not simple: attend an elite school. For graduates from most elite colleges, the unemployment statistics are less relevant. A degree from school like Harvard or Oxford likely helps you get a job, even if it's not a job you want. Top-ranked schools also tend to have strong alumni networks that you can tap into. If you have the option to attend an elite school and if it makes sense for you financially (this is a big "if"), I say go for it. It is hard to envision that "Harvard" on your résumé could be a bad thing. The value of these brands will prove themselves time and again in your career. The trouble, however, may be getting into an elite institution in the first place. Admissions rates have been steadily declining. Harvard, for example, admitted only 5.9 percent of applicants for its class of 2018—and that wasn't even the lowest admission rate in the U.S.[5]

While unemployment rates might be lower for graduates of these colleges, you don't have to attend an elite school in order to have a successful and fulfilling career. If getting into an elite school isn't a reality for you, don't worry—it isn't for most of us! The second path to making sure your degree is a good investment is even more effective. Because of shifting demand in the job market, graduates with certain degrees have higher rates of full-time employment postgraduation. For example, the U.S. Department of Education's National Center for Information Statistics released a study in 2009 showing unemployment by discipline for 2007–08 bachelor's degree graduates. While overall unemployment was at 9 percent for this group of recent grads, that number shifted based on the area of study. Computer and information sciences or engineering majors had much lower levels of unemployment, 6 percent and 5 percent respectively. Those who completed health-care-related (6 percent) and education (5 percent) majors were also below the average. However, graduates with degrees in the social sciences (12 percent) and humanities (13 percent) had much higher levels of unemployment.[6]

Looking beyond the data, how many times have you heard a liberal arts graduate joke that his PhD in history is going to make him unemployable after school? Again, I am not telling you not to major in history. There are plenty of viable professions one can enter with a history degree, but know what those are instead of just crossing your fingers. Not having a plan is simply going to cause you more anxiety as you look toward a clouded future. Do your research and have ideas about where that degree can take you.

There is also no shame in choosing a job or field of study tied to a growing industry where there will be a demand for talent. Notice above that the STEM (science, technology, engineering, mathematics) disciplines have particularly high demand for graduates following school.

So what does all this mean for you (or for the young people in your life)? Back to my original point: *as you choose a degree, be informed about what the market looks like after graduation—and for the next decade and beyond.* Unless you have money from family means, the reality is that you must be able to pay back loans (if you have them) and you must be able to support yourself in the lifestyle you want. If you would like to major in art history, do so, but recognize some of the earnings trade-offs you might be making. When I was younger, my dream car was a Porsche 911—and I wanted it before I turned thirty (yes, I realize it sounds shallow, but hey!). Majoring in philosophy wasn't necessarily going to put me on the quick path to getting that Porsche.

A final thought on undergraduate education: perhaps you read the statistic "half of graduates will work jobs that don't require degrees" and then considered the burgeoning levels of student debt (as of 2012, undergraduate debt per person averaged $29,400).[7] There's a chance you thought: If a degree doesn't guarantee a job but pretty much guarantees debt, why get one? I am all for people pursuing higher education. The data is pretty firmly on the side of getting a college degree (the unemployment rate in 2014 for people with a college degree was 3.5 percent, while it was 6 percent for people with only a high school education; earning power also increases dramatically for degree holders).[8] However, I recognize that a degree is not always a prerequisite for success.

There are successful entrepreneurs who created companies without a college education, although not many (think Steve Jobs and Bill Gates). Additionally, many careers don't require a four-year degree and still have earning potential. Trade schools and apprenticeships are viable options for a high-earning career; you just have to be smart about it. The highest-earning careers that don't require a four-year degree change from year to year. The U.S. Bureau of Labor Statistics is an excellent resource, offering data on more than forty professions—like registered nurse, air traffic controller, and radiation therapist—that pay well over $58,000 a year on average.[9] You also don't have to go to college right after high school. If you would like to take time to work and get more experience before launching into your education that is perfectly fine as well. My message is that you are best served by making your education work for you rather than blindly following the norms. What you study, what degrees you need, and when you get those degrees are all part of an evolving plan of which you are the administrator.

Your Education Does Not End with Graduation

Continuing education is an important part of any discussion about career preparation—your education does not end with your undergraduate studies. Continuing education means anything from getting a formal graduate degree to taking online classes. After working for several years, I got my MBA and a postgraduate diploma, and participated in three executive education programs (I finally got the opportunity to get my Harvard education through executive development). Getting a professional degree like an MBA or JD is clearly a big decision with complicated financial aspects. There isn't a blanket answer to the question of whether you should pursue such a degree, but you can do a basic investment analysis to help determine the worth of the degree. This is easy: simply take the cost of your degree and then find data for what your projected earnings would be in the new position you could get. Don't forget to factor in the estimated opportunity cost of earnings lost during the time you will be in school or neglect to look at what your earnings would be even if you didn't get the degree. Is it worth it? The average payback time for students in my MBA program was three years, so the math made sense for me.

Even if a formal graduate or professional degree isn't right for you, consider taking part in a short-course executive education program. These programs are usually specialized in a certain discipline and tend to be very practical. If you are interested in taking one of these, do a quick search online. Many established universities offer executive education programs. Online courses that are open to everyone are even less of a commitment. Choose a topic that interests you, like basic accounting or advanced Excel, and sign up! Many companies will reimburse you for the cost of the course if you can make a clear case for the business value your new skills will add. If you are reentering the workforce after an absence (like family leave), online courses offer a great way to brush up on your skill set without needing to go to school full time. Some people in this position take classes periodically while they are at home to keep their brains engaged in the business world.

The message here is that you should never stop learning and growing. Your career will benefit from a mindset of both curiosity and discipline. Even if you are not enrolled in a class, make time to read business books or keep up with publications like *Forbes,* the *Harvard Business Review,* and the *Wall Street Journal.* Knowledge of the macroeconomic climate will help you be more effective in your career. What you learn in your reading can be great conversation points at work or networking events. Over time, this knowledge will aid your decision making and will increase other people's perception of your intellectual capability.

Your First Job—Is It Forever?

If you are about to graduate from college and are beginning the search for your first full-time job, you are at a unique point in your career. The plentiful options in front of you can be over-whelming. You may feel like you are irreversibly committing to a job and lifestyle. All my advice up to this point has been about the importance of strategic planning. But before you put huge amounts of pressure on yourself, sit back and realize that your first job isn't forever. The first real job you have is an important stepping-stone on your professional journey, but it most likely won't define what you do for the rest of your life.

If you are ambitious, is it helpful if this first step is a strategic one? The answer is yes, but you can make any job experience valuable as long as you are smart about it. If you didn't get that plum banking job you desperately wanted, don't worry. This doesn't mean you aren't going to have the career you want. You just have to figure out a different way to reach your goals. Perhaps you take a position with a smaller firm, or maybe you find a job with a high-growth financial services start-up. Maybe you get a graduate degree in statistics. The point is that there are plenty of options available to you. Choose one that will set you up well for the next step and get going!

Some grads don't go right into a career track and instead

choose to take several years to travel or pursue some other endeavor. Spending a year backpacking in Europe might not put you on the fastest management track, but you can find ways to translate that experience into marketable skills when you interview for jobs. You could talk about the problem-solving skills you learned, how handy you've become at administering schedules on tight budgets, or the interpersonal skills you developed negotiating in different cultural contexts. You can be nonlinear about your path as long as you are smart in describing the experience later.

Sometimes a little work experience can help you refine your vision of your career path: jobs that show you what you *don't* want to do can be as useful as jobs you like. An advanced degree like an MBA is a good way to learn this as well. Taking classes offers a low-risk way to pinpoint interests. When I was getting my MBA, most of my classmates were headed into finance. Getting exposure to their world was a helpful way to learn that wasn't what I wanted to do. However, I was intrigued by the entrepreneurial bent of some of these professionals—starting a business seemed like something I could do, and do well! Internships also offer you a short-term opportunity to evaluate whether a career or company is right for you (but keep in mind they do not always pay well, and some don't pay at all).

My final word of caution about the beginning of your career is that there seems to be a new belief that the first decade of your career doesn't matter at all. This is not true. While your first job out of school probably won't be the thing you do forever, your twenties are not wasted time (there is a great TED Talk by Meg Jay).[10] As I've said, your twenties are for refining your career vision, figuring out what you want, and getting started on that path. The earlier you can do this, the better. There are plenty of examples of young people in their twenties and early thirties who run huge companies. Think about Mark Zuckerberg of Facebook, Daniel Schwartz of Burger King, or Kat Cole of Cinnabon.

Your Next First Job: Reentering the Workforce

People enter and exit the workforce for many reasons, including sabbaticals and family leaves. The most common reason people step out of their careers, other than retirement, is to raise children full time. Both men and women can become stay-at-home parents, but the responsibility falls to women especially. The statistics on women who choose to exit the workforce are staggering: 74 percent of women who take time out to start a family will return, but only 40 percent of those will end up working full time.[11] This is surprising, considering that 93 percent of women express an intention to return. Either priorities shift or reentry is just too difficult.

The reality is that extended leave from any job has an opportunity cost. For people who do want to come back to work, reentering the workforce can be more complicated than entering in the first place. If you left to raise children, those kids are going to limit your flexibility—or at least change it. Working hundred-hour weeks like you did when you were twenty-five may no longer be an option (we will address time management in more detail in the next chapter). Even if you are used to a fast-paced work environment, such long workweeks may no longer fit your lifestyle. Finding a job that allows telecommuting or doesn't prioritize face time are options. Other people who find themselves in this position become consultants or start their own businesses so they have more control over their schedules (more on starting your own business in chapter 8, "Taking Action and Risks"). Many professionals at senior levels have a spouse who has a less demanding job—or at the least, the couple splits the child-care and household responsibilities evenly.

Additionally, unlike a new graduate, if you are reentering the workforce you have valuable work experience and a skill set. However, in the time you have taken off, you run the risk that your skills have gone stale. Technology moves quickly. Knowing, for example, how to use the latest computer program in your field is important. Before you interview for jobs, figure out areas where you may be lacking proficiency and take a class or two to freshen your skills. You can even meet with a coach who can help you do a holistic assessment and prescribe methods to strengthen your current skills.

I tell people who are looking to take an extended family leave to *always leave one foot in the door*. For example, if you can work on a freelance basis, as a consultant, or two Fridays a month—do it. If you have the option, try working in the family business keeping books, helping with marketing, or handling office administration. Get involved with community boards or political projects that appeal to you. Start a small business like an eBay store, or sell Mary Kay cosmetics. Take classes. Just do *something* that keeps you in the game! Regardless of the income you earn, staying in the workforce on any level will make returning full time much easier. Even if you are not sure you will ever work full time again, having the option to do so is invaluable.

Full-time parents who are planning to return to work once their kids head off for university will need to think outside the box. Many people, especially women, feel their only recourse is to work in retail. While this is not bad, it might be quite different from what you did before having kids. I am not trying to be discouraging, so let me be clear: if you are interested in rejoining the workforce, you can find opportunities no matter how long you have been away. But be aware that the more time you take away from work, the harder it is to return to a traditional job. If you have an inkling that salaried work will be something you are interested in doing in the future, find ways to be involved professionally, or even in the community, that keep building your experience.

Keeping a Foot in the Door

Reena has been practicing law for twenty-four years. When it came to balancing the kids' needs and her full-time job at a demanding, big-name law firm, Reena realized she couldn't do both. Many female lawyers end up opting out of the workforce altogether, but Reena wasn't ready to give up her career. Her solution? She decided to go "in-house" (meaning that she kept her credentials active but didn't practice) and started to serve on various boards. Her company was happy to keep her in this capacity in the hope that she would return full time. Once her kids were older, Reena started working full time again, and was able to pick up where she'd left off.

Putting It All Together

It can be difficult to have a truly big-picture perspective on planning your career. Though many people don't think about this, your professional journey doesn't start with the first day of your first job—it starts with your education. It is hard to be mindful about stepping out of the professional world when you are fully immersed in it, and it's hard to think about going back when you're focused on raising your kids or enjoying your long-term sabbatical. But these are big pieces of every career road map, pieces that set the stage for everything you will do after.

Planning is not just about that next step on the career ladder, it's about setting the stage for moves you will make ten or fifteen years down the line. When you have your goals well defined, you will find it easier to pay attention to how your education ties into your larger ambitions. And by making smart choices about your education or first job, you are establishing good habits. You are stepping away from the mentor myth and setting a solid course for your own career path.

CHAPTER 3

A Week Is 168 Hours—Use Them Wisely

Perhaps you read the previous chapter and were thinking, "Yes! I would love to sit down and think through a compre hensive career plan...if I only had the time." This is a complaint I hear over and over, both from people I work with and from my friends. It doesn't matter whether you're a working parent, a stay-at-home parent, or single—the sentiment is the same: there are not enough hours in the day. Think about how many business books focus exclusively on time manage ment. No career strategy, however great it is, will help you succeed unless you make the time to implement it.

I recently read a book, *Overwhelmed* by Brigid Schulte, that does an excellent job breaking down this problem.[1] Schulte hypothesizes that in the Western world we are obsessed with "busyness." How busy you are shows how important your time is. The problem with valuing busyness is that the demands on the modern professional's time are already immense. Work, kids, friends, working out, philanthropy, helping aging parents, hobbies—where does it end? I truly do think the juggling is harder for people with children, but those without kids have it rough as well. Expectations are high on all fronts.

The reality is that if you want a successful career, you're going to be busy. Whether you're a corporate executive with little flexibility or you run an eBay store and make your own hours, there's no escaping the fact that work is going to take up a lot of time. Part of the issue is that technology has enabled us to work wherever we are, resulting in long hours. Most people are connected to their e-mail every waking hour. Video chatting with a client in Hong Kong at 9 p.m. is now a perfectly normal occurrence; in fact, I had two conference calls completed before seven this morning with clients in South Africa and France. My iPhone, personal computer, and work computer keep me connected 24–7. If you want to work all the time, or if your manager expects you to, there are no logistical barriers. This is the reality of modern professional life (BlackBerry briefly tried to market a separate "work" and "personal" mode for their devices, but it sold terribly).

You can either reject this reality and choose a lifestyle that better accommodates your priorities or accept that a serious career will take time, and plan accordingly by integrating your professional and personal lives. This chapter discusses a three-part solution to managing your time: establishing your priorities, planning your schedule, and learning to be flexible. I can't fix your demanding schedule, but I can help you make it more productive and easier to live with.

Solution Part 1: Establishing Priorities

How many articles or books have you read that debate whether people (especially women) can "have it all"? I've lost count at this point. "Having it all" means a wide spectrum of things: a fulfilling career, an energizing social life, kids (for some), and time to pursue your interests. Which do you prioritize? Managing priorities is especially complicated if you have kids (your friends you can ignore for weeks at a time, your kids not so much). Is it possible to maintain a high-momentum career after having kids? On one side of this question you have rallying cries for people to stay in the workforce after having children and on the other you have people who feel that the current setup of our institutions makes staying home once you have a child a near necessity rather than a choice. Many women even feel that the question of "how they do it all" is offensive (famously, Tina Fey).[2] After all, it's not something professionally successful men are often asked.

Choosing to stay home or to continue a professional career is not a black-and-white matter; while everyone who wants to both work and have a family should ideally be able to, every circumstance is unique. For example, some people (women especially) have a spouse who doesn't want them to work. In many cases, however, a discussion of a stay-at-home spouse isn't even relevant, as many families don't have the financial wherewithal to allow one parent to leave the workforce. In order to feed their families and keep a roof over their heads, both parents must be employed. For other people, working is a choice rather than a necessity, but they would like to weight more time toward raising their children.

The point is that your priorities will always be shifting. Devoting lots of time to being successful in one area of your life might mean another area isn't getting the attention you would like to give it. Even if you don't have children, there are probably many things you would like to be doing with your time that your work hours don't allow for. I could spend all day making business calls or perfecting my golf swing, but either way, I wouldn't see my kids. When I take a vacation or spend the day at one of my kid's field trips, my work has to take a backseat. Life balance is a mercurial, subjective concept. I am lucky. I believe I can have all the things I want—just not always in the proportions I want them. At some points, work needs more of my attention and my time teeter-totter shifts in that direction. At other points, my kids need more of my time. Owning and running a business and having kids are both described as "full-time" pursuits but there is only one of me. Today I might be 60 percent CEO and 40 percent mom but tomorrow those percentages might be different, and that has to be good enough.

What I'm talking about is the ability to keep perspective on what is important to you and how much you can do with limited amounts of time. Planning your schedule isn't about fitting in more and more stuff. Many people already do that to the point of collapse. It's about knowing your priorities and spending your time as you wish, in a way that meets your objectives. That's what "having it all" truly means. After reading this chapter, you might even decide to *remove* items from your schedule. Your time is valuable. Every item that goes into your schedule needs to be assessed against your priorities.

Ask yourself what is most important to you in this moment, and how that fits into your long-term goals. I would like to be a successful mother *and* an entrepreneur—how am I going to make that work? What does it mean for me today, and a year from now? Figure out what your priorities are and allow yourself a little room for imperfection. On the days it all seems to fall apart, don't worry—this is reality for most of us. I would need a whole other book to share my "bad mommy" moments, including a recent day when I was in such a rush I handed my son one of my black skirts instead of his jacket for an awards banquet. Needless to say, it was embarrassing for him to be walking around with one of my skirts, and he was also pretty cold. You can't have it all, all the time. On the days you strike a balance you're happy with, take a moment and appreciate your success.

Solution Part 2: Planning Your Schedule

I recently had lunch with Jeff Immelt, who is currently recognized as one of the world's most important CEOs (at the time of writing, General Electric has a market cap of over $250 billion). We spent quite a bit of time discussing the importance of investing in human capital, career development, and personal success factors. A key factor of success he mentioned is the ability to manage time. He was emphatic about using time wisely and putting everything he does on the clock, which he felt was truly the best way to keep track of where time goes.

Many people talk about not having enough hours in the day to accomplish everything they want. This might be true, but most don't take advantage of all the hours available to them. There are 168 hours in a week, and the key to unlocking the full potential of all those hours is great planning.

Business guru Brian Tracy famously said, "Every minute you spend in planning saves ten minutes in execution."[3] I find this to be absolutely true in my own life. The strange thing is that I don't encounter many people who take the time to plan their schedules thoughtfully. Plenty of executives I know let assistants dictate their schedules for them, and they spend their unplanned time putting out fires. Many people barrel through their week without really knowing where their time goes. This can be dissatisfying. You might be busy every minute, yet you don't accomplish the things you want to. I know lots of people who are so exhausted by the end of the day that the only thing they feel like doing at night is watching TV, which—though entertaining—isn't usually listed as one of our top priorities.

The first step in planning your 168 hours is taking a high-level view of where your time goes. Whatever your other priorities, there are certain things you *must* do—small things like sleeping and eating. A useful exercise is to journal your time for a week and then take an honest look at where you're spending it. How much TV do you really watch? Are you spending an excessive amount of time answering e-mails? Assess your bad habits and, using the advice in this chapter, make a plan for the good habits you're going to incorporate into your schedule. Time is an abstract concept, so plotting your week in writing will make clear to you where all those hours are going. Planning should be a continual process, but setting aside thirty minutes every Sunday to sketch your new and improved weekly schedule will be a huge boon to you. You should be able to do the things most important to you— you just have to own your priorities and have the discipline to stick to your plans.

The Eight "Time" Categories

I view time as falling into eight categories: sleeping, eating, hygiene, commuting, work, working out, family/friends time, and general leisure. The first four categories are nonnegotiable unless you work exclusively from home, in which case commute time is not a factor. Based on my own estimates, these four categories alone average about seventy hours per week.

So what are you going to do with the remaining ninety-eight hours? Let's say you work "normal" hours—strictly forty hours a week. That leaves you with a full fifty-eight hours in which to live the rest of your life. This would be ideal, but most people spend about 50 percent of their waking time working, or just over sixty hours a week (this includes commuting and returning calls and e-mails during off hours). That's twenty hours less that you can spend socializing, cleaning your house, working out, or pursuing hobbies. Realistically, early in your career you will probably be putting in extra amounts of work, especially if you work billable hours as a consultant, lawyer, or accountant. It's not unheard of for starting analysts at big investment banks or consulting firms to work one hundred-hour weeks.

Leisure time is the category in which people really get shortchanged (again Schulte's *Overwhelmed* does a masterful job exploring this topic). This is especially true when it comes to women's time. Studies previously showed that women, on average, have about thirty hours of leisure time a week.[4] But when you take a deeper look at those thirty hours, they are typically fragmented into small, harried chunks: twenty minutes here, fifteen minutes there. Most of that time is squeezed between coffee meetings and kids' baseball practice drop-offs. Therefore, the kind of leisure time women get is designated as "contaminated time"—time that's not especially useful or relaxing unless you intentionally plan useful things that fit logically into small blocks of time.[5]

No matter how creative you get with your planning, it's hard to escape these general categories. But you can employ high-level strategies that help you allocate time in line with your priorities. You can also get creative with how you use your time within these categories.

Keeping One Calendar

The foundation of all time management strategies is viewing your calendar holistically. Many people I know parse their time into "professional" and "personal" chunks, keeping separate calendars for each category. Not to be obvious, but time is time. Put all your appointments on the same calendar, and categorize from there. It's impossible to know where your time is really going unless you assess it all at once. This will prevent you from double-booking yourself or arranging work and personal events too close together. Share that mega-calendar with the people who most impact it, whether that's your partner, assistant, or colleagues (there's a handy function on most digital calendaring systems that allows you to make the details of events visible only to certain people). They'll have a better view of where your time goes as well, and can help in planning. In my case, my husband knows to send calendar updates and invites for his business trips or work engagements he would like me to attend to my master calendar.

Planning for Impact

My second piece of high-level scheduling advice is to optimize for impact. What does this mean? Whether in your professional or personal life, instead of maxing out the amount of time you can spend doing something, you should strive for quality.

Let's first discuss maximizing your impact in your work life. In any office, you want to be "known." This sounds Machiavellian but is pretty innocent. You won't get nominated for projects or get face time with management unless people know you work at the company and remember who you are. There are different ways to achieve this exposure. I know many people who believe they must be the first at their desk every day and the last to leave at night. You *can* do this—but it's not the most effective way to spend your time. Instead of putting in tons of extra hours, *vary the hours you work*. Key figures will arrive at or leave work at different times. You want to have as broad an acquaintance base as possible at work, and changing the times you work will give you a chance to encounter the largest number of colleagues without having to be at the office all the time.

Another strategy you can employ—and again, I'm not advocating creepy behavior—is to figure out when the CEO or other executives arrive or leave. Time your coming and going with theirs. Not every day (that's stalking), but often enough that you can have a few key encounters. Networking happens in odd places, like the parking lot or lobby, so maximize your chances of bumping elbows with execs. Being recognizable and remembered is more important than simply grinding out the longest hours and hoping someone notices. I can't even count the number of meetings I've been in where the CEO says, "What about the woman in marketing who sits next to Diana?" or "Is that the guy from the elevator with the red briefcase?" I've even seen the "longest hours" attitude backfire—instead of being known as the most committed colleague, the person who's always at his desk is either seen as inefficient or as having a concerning lack of other stuff to do.

Planning for impact is important in your personal life as well. While women on average still spend more time with children than men do, men have begun to take on a more active parenting role.[6] However, fathers' time with kids tends to differ in nature than mothers' time. Fathers get to do more of the "fun" activities.[7] There's something to be said for this. An hour spent nagging the kids to clean their rooms or cleaning their rooms yourself does not count as spending time with them. One way around this is—you guessed it— planning. Have fun activities lined up that you want to do, and put household chores in a category separate from "family time" (maybe even use chore charts to create a group effort).

Outsourcing is another good option. We tend to view services provided by babysitters, house cleaners, or personal chefs as something only the very wealthy can afford. However, the hourly rate of the service provider might be well worth the time freed up. Outsourcing the unimportant tasks can be an important investment for you. There are great free apps and tools that help you figure out the hourly value of your time, and these can help you decide whether it makes sense to outsource certain tasks (I like the "Value of Your Time Calculator" offered by Clearer Thinking at www.clearer thinking.org).

Leveraging the Power of Multipliers

A technique I believe in strongly is leveraging the power of multipliers. What does this mean? A multiplier is "a single activity that... fulfills multiple goals."[8] This differs from multitasking because you are performing a single activity and are fully present for that one task, rather than trying to do many things at once. For example, instead of going for a jog and then meeting a friend for coffee, why not go for a jog with your friend? Instead of letting your commute be wasted time, listen to a podcast, relevant news, or language tapes. Leveraging the power of multipliers lets you accomplish more by overlaying tasks that make sense together.

Setting Your Default to "No"

Sometimes it seems that we are hardwired to say *yes* to the many requests people make of us, whether that's helping others, going to events, taking on other people's workloads, showing up to flag football, making cookies for book club, and so on. When you are invited to an event, what is your reaction? When I am invited to a professional event, I can usually rationalize it as a good networking opportunity. And of course I like to do fun things with my friends and family, so I want to accept most of the personal invitations, too. This is not a great time management practice. As accommodating and enthusiastic as you may be, saying yes to everything makes organizing a schedule difficult, especially if you are struggling to keep things under control.

The solution? Set your default to *no*. For any request made of you, mentally assign it a "no can do" from the outset. Then, compare the request against your list of priorities to see if it aligns with something important to you. If the request is to attend a professional event on a Friday night and you had pledged to spend that time with family, then it remains a *no*. If it is a conference that requires travel but features a large number of CEOs in your industry, maybe it becomes a *yes*.

This applies to work projects as well. Many people volunteer for tasks that don't fall strictly within the definition of their job. This is a fine line. On one hand, you want to be an enthusiastic go-getter; on the other, you don't want to get mired in work that isn't yours and won't help promote you. I don't mean that you should only take flashy assignments; just be strategic about what you're saying *yes* to. For example, don't always offer to take the lunch order or the minutes in a meeting. Instead, volunteer to head a major initiative or lead a task force—don't let a lack of confidence hold you back. The latter two tasks showcase your abilities rather than your "niceness." Office "housework" in general isn't a strategic thing to spend time doing. Don't make extra work for anyone, but emptying trashcans, washing coffee mugs, and cleaning the bathroom is not a strategic use of your time. I am not telling you to be a snob or to be entitled about having a clean workspace, but there's a danger, especially if you are a woman, in routinely assuming those tasks.

I've had many people tell me that defaulting to "no" has been life changing for them. Being able to say *no* or *yes* when they wanted allowed them to make better decisions and focus on the things with the highest impact for themselves, their families, and their careers. Acknowledge that your time is limited and not everything will fit. Embrace discipline and be highly selective about how you fill all parts of your schedule.

Establishing Routines

I realize that establishing default habits and routines sounds boring, but it is a highly effective method of organizing your schedule. The less planning you have to do and the less time you spend making low-impact decisions, the better. In your work life, this perhaps means that you hold recurring meetings at the same time (i.e., staff meetings are always Wednesday morning at ten). Establishing habits as simple as leaving your keys and wallet in the same place is highly effective— imagine how many hours people spend every week looking for those pesky car keys. I was always guilty of this until my five-year-old daughter thoughtfully made a container for my keys—it's ironic that it sometimes takes a five-year-old to point out obvious time wasters.

When I travel, I have a default routine I follow. I happen to travel quite a lot for work. As anyone who travels knows, it's easy to get off track with diet and exercise. In order to keep my sanity, as soon as I reserve my flights I book a 6 a.m. spin class near my hotel, look up the closest Chipotle, and pack my protein shakes. This way, I know my workouts won't fall off, and I can have healthy food for all the meals that aren't scheduled. For me, this planning helps offset some of the damage wrought by the restaurant and conference food, and it reduces the time I would spend trying to decide where to eat and when to workout.

Managing Your Personal Life

To continue to drill down on schedule planning, let's take a quick look at some tips you can use to optimize your time in your personal life. Most people avoid planning in their personal lives out of fear of killing spontaneity or flexibility. Don't worry. Being a little less spontaneous is worth the increased quality of life.

Sleep

Most type-A achievers at some point in their lives begin to rationalize long, late nights coupled with early mornings. We believe that we're just too busy to sleep. And how much sleep do we need anyway? Truthfully, a lot. Most people require seven to eight hours of sleep every night. The drawbacks of too little sleep have been proven time and time again. If you aren't well rested, you will be less energetic, less able to focus and perform complex thinking, and probably less pleasant to be around.

Perhaps you only sleep five hours a night in order to fit in that last bit of e-mail every night or to get a jump on the work-day in the morning because you consider yourself one of the exceptions. You could be what is called a "short sleeper," but know two things: first, being able to sleep less is a genetic condition based on a mutation of the hDEC2 gene. It is esti-mated that only about 1 percent of the population has this mutation.[9] Second, if you're sleeping less than seven to eight hours a night and you don't have this mutation, you're not hard core, you're just less effective at work.

The best way to ensure you get enough sleep is to—wait for it—establish a sleep routine and stick to it. Try to go to bed at the same time every night and get up at the same time every morning. Getting little sleep during the week and sleeping in on weekends isn't as good for you as getting a solid seven to eight hours every night. Don't succumb to the temptations of late-night television surfing or social media wandering. It's not worth the trade-off. Some people like to take power naps in the afternoon if they haven't gotten much sleep the night before. If your employer is comfortable with that, go for it. However, the best way to have full use of your mental capacities is to get enough sleep at regular times on a daily basis.

Fitness

The first thing to go, for busy people, is fitness. Office work generally doesn't lend itself to a fit lifestyle. People sit for long hours and develop dietary habits that are unhealthy. Being fit is important, though, and not just for your long-term health—fitness matters for your personal presentation. I will devote a whole chapter to this concept later, but like it or not, image matters in the corporate world. Staying on top of your game in terms of your appearance will make you a more marketable employee. Some people mistakenly believe that getting exercise will be draining, but being fit actually gives you more energy to apply toward your work and your day.[10]

The best way to remain fit is to get into an established workout routine. It should become second nature to you, like sleeping or eating, to get some kind of exercise during the day. A good way to make sure this happens is to plan workouts that are on your way home, on your way to work, or during lunch (personally, I vary my schedule among the three, depending on the day of the week). You don't have to make an extra trip from the office or from your home to your gym; it's easy to just stop off on the way and get your workout done without adding extra commute time. This is also a great area for leveraging the power of multipliers. Twice a week, I drop my son off at football practice and go for a run at the same facility. For the rest of my workouts, I schedule two training sessions in the morning on the way to work, bike ride with my kids, and go to spin class a couple of times a week with a colleague—we then plan to meet at a nearby coffee shop right afterward in lieu of a meeting at the office.

There are things you can do during the workday, too, like making sure to always take stairs or go for a walk at lunchtime. If you or your employer is willing to invest, you can get treadmill desks (I have one and love it) or use a balance ball for a chair to minimize bad posture. I even know a few people who take walks during one-on-one meetings rather than sitting in a conference room. You might not have the flexibility or capital to do this, but these are small ways to incorporate fitness into your day. My latest trick is to book hotels that, for a nominal fee, will put a treadmill or spin bike in your room.

Diet

This is not a nutrition book (thank goodness), so I am not going to tell you what you should or should not be eating. My diet advice here is simple and relates only to time management: plan your meals and pack lunches as often as possible.

While meals are often used for networking, it is difficult to eat out and order healthily (plus, this can become expensive). Packing meals saves time deciding what you're going to eat and gives you control over nutrition.

This may sound boring to some, but I eat the same foods for breakfast and lunch every day, and our dinner menu is the same each night of the week (i.e., we have a Monday night dinner that we repeat every week, and so on). If I don't have an event at night, having a meal already planned saves me the time I would spend deciding what to eat, planning the rest of the meal, and shopping for ingredients. I know this seems rigid, but I can't begin to explain the hassle it saves us. Plus, the whole family loves Monday sushi night and Friday taco night.

Managing Your Professional Life

There are many strategies for optimizing your time at work, and lots of great books have been written by business gurus who specialize in this area. Some experts have made entire careers out of lecturing on time management. Exploring all the professional time management strategy available is beyond the scope of this book, however I've put together a few handy tips from my own work experience and experiences shared with me by the people I work with. I believe every professional can use these strategies to make their work time more manageable.

Meetings

Meetings are meant to be a collaborative time in which decisions are made communally and efficiently. Often, though, without a skilled person to run them, meetings become mired in meandering conversation or arguments and take up valuable time they don't need to. Absent an excellent moderator, meetings can still be run efficiently if ground rules are established at the outset.

First, meetings should last no more than thirty minutes. Of course there will be a few exceptions, like quarterly board meetings. But in general, meetings stop being effective if they are more than thirty minutes. Keeping the time window short inspires efficiency. If you have so much material to discuss or so many decisions to make that you require more than thirty minutes, have two meetings.

Often, I find that the person in charge of moderating the meeting lets it run over if the discussion has not ended. This should not happen. If meetings are scheduled for thirty minutes, then there is a hard stop at the time everyone agreed to. Letting meetings run long shows poor time management and is disrespectful to attendees. If a manager is running a meeting and decides to go over the allotted time, a subordinate who had something scheduled in that next time slot may be uncomfortable speaking up and reminding the manager of the schedule. In my own company, I make sure meeting overrun doesn't happen by intentionally scheduling meetings back to back, so they can't run long (and then no one has the terrible job of timing me).

A good way to prevent endless discussions and meeting overrun is to circulate an agenda that everyone can read in advance of the meeting. Once the meeting begins, address each point on the agenda in a concise way. Whenever possible, avoid introducing agenda points at the meetings—if an item is not on the list of previously agreed upon material, it doesn't get discussed. The point of circulating the agenda before the meeting, other than to keep the discussion on track, is to help attendees participate more effectively. Many people require time to absorb information before they can ask meaningful questions or make effective decisions. If you bring up items out of the blue, you run the risk of blindsiding people. As an added bonus, an agreed-upon agenda gives you time to over-prepare and look like a star.

As the meeting progresses, accountability lists should be made so that decisions aren't lost. This is also a good way to keep the meeting focused by reminding everyone that you are there for a purpose.

E-Mail and Internet Use

E-mail is both the bane and blessing of every professional's existence. Managing your e-mail is key to keeping your professional time management on track. The first thing you need to do is turn off the pop-up notifications on your e-mail client or phone. Incredible amounts of time are wasted by endless e-mail checking. You might be in the middle of a task but then—ping!—the notification is too hard to ignore and you head back to your inbox, only to get pulled into a different endeavor. On average, interruptions last about six to nine minutes with a follow-up four to five minutes of recovery time needed before you can get back on track.[11] Just four or five interruptions are enough to kill a whole hour!

This kind of context switching is terribly inefficient. The key to defeating endless e-mail review is to establish times to check your e-mail: morning, midday, and the end of your workday. Don't worry if people are used to receiving responses from you right away. As you develop new habits, you will reset expectations.

One of the worst e-mail habits is using your inbox as a to-do list. I understand why people default to this practice; your inbox is a natural repository for the daily requests you get. But this is a self-defeating practice. E-mails often get lost, buried beneath the deluge of new e-mails you are constantly getting. And then, there goes the to-do item. It is also hard to arrange e-mail to-dos in the right levels of priority. How do you know which to do first? A much better practice is to take the e-mail request and turn it into a to-do item on your list of priorities. You can even write a note to yourself to follow up on the original e-mail once you have completed the task.

With regard to general Internet and mobile device use, be mindful of the amount of time you are spending surfing the Internet, checking social media, and texting or chatting. The ten-minute chunks you spend might not feel like a lot considered separately, but they add up and take focus away from your task at hand. The time and effort you spend refocusing after each interruption is an additional loss. I am not saying you should never take breaks; by all means allot some time to let your brain rest. You may decide that every hour you will spend five minutes clearing your head by checking in with a friend or your spouse or by reading a newsfeed. But once you choose a strategy for your breaks, resist distractions during your dedicated work time.

Setting Goals

Your daily mantra should be: "Today I will be successful if I achieve…". Having a to-do list is a great practice, but you shouldn't arrange your day by blindly checking items off the list. At the start of the day, ask yourself, "If today is going to be really effective, what will I have accomplished by the end of the day?" Don't leave work until you have finished the goals you set for yourself. Framing your day with a tangible productivity goal is an excellent way to keep yourself focused (procrastination is too easy, with the Internet wide open to us). This mindset will help you make sure that you finish tasks in a day, rather than starting them and then leaving them hanging indefinitely. The best part is that—because they know what they're supposed to be accomplishing and avoid procrastinating—people who subscribe to this approach tend to work fewer hours. Who doesn't like shorter days? The added benefit is leaving the office knowing you've had a successful day rather than leaving with a half-completed, four-page to-do list.

Follow-Up Tasks

After ingesting the information above, you might like to try some exercises to sharpen your time management skills. I am a big fan of the late Randy Pausch, a lecturer at Carnegie Mellon University. One particular lecture focused on time management, and came with a handy set of exercises you can do on your own to get some time management practice (you can find the lecture at www.cs.cmu.edu/~pausch/).

The first exercise is to start using your calendar—if you don't have one, get a Day-Timer or other such planner. Old-fashioned paper planners seem to have fallen out of fashion, with the invention of iPhones and the rest of our digital gadgets, but I think it is important to write out a schedule. If you prefer a digital calendar, go ahead and use that, but be diligent about entering information into it.

The second exercise is to start ordering your to-do list by priority, not by the date you got the task. This way, you know what to take care of first—because it's the first thing on the list! I also like using the Eisenhower Method as laid out in Stephen Covey's *First Things First*.[12] Tasks are categorized into one of four quadrants: important/urgent, important/not urgent, not important/not urgent, and not important/urgent. Using this method, you can avoid the "urgency" pit that many of us fall into, wherein we focus our efforts on the deadlines that are fast approaching (even if we aren't accomplishing much) instead of focusing on long-term time management.

Solution Part 3: Learning to Be Flexible

Part of planning is learning how to roll with the punches. How did poet Robert Burns put it? "The best laid plans..."— and I am sure you can fill in the rest from experience. Knowing that your plans may be interrupted isn't a reason to forgo planning. But you can't be rigid about all your scheduling all the time. Sometimes unforeseen circumstances arise, and all the anticipation in the world isn't going to help you plan around them.

Knowing your short-term demands and long-term priorities is a great way to keep your head when your plans are disrupted by a sick child or a demanding client. Your schedule will be a constantly evolving beast. If you're not sure which item on your to-do list is the most important, assess both its importance and its urgency, or revisit your four-quadrant tool. When your plans begin to unravel, just look at your priority list and reformat as needed.

You can also build more flexibility into your schedule.

More and more professionals today choose to telecommute, which means they work from home but are available by phone or e-mail. Others work from home every Friday or on special occasions. The trick is to get your manager to sign off on this in advance. Establish expectations at the outset about how you can be contacted and what your deliverables will be.

If working from home isn't an option for you, you can try limiting your hours to your optimal productive hours. Most people can really only focus on work for about six hours a day. I believe people aren't productive after a thirty-seven-hour workweek. In my own company, Inspired HR, there are no set hours during which employees are required to be in the office. People work on projects or take calls from home, but are much more productive and happy than when they're required to sit at their desk for twelve hours a day.

Working as a consultant or owning your own business can also lead to more flexible hours. Full-time corporate jobs often emphasize face time at the office. If you transition your professional experience into work as a consultant, you can gain more control over the hours you work. Be warned, though: some small business owners or consultants work extra-long hours! Choosing one of these paths does not guarantee flexibility. You need to consciously create a consulting practice or business with hours that are negotiable.

An important element of flexibility is having people who can help you out in your personal life. If you have kids, this is vital. *Lean In* by Sheryl Sandberg has a great chapter titled "Make Your Partner an Equal Partner." The title is self-explanatory: make sure your partner shares equally in domestic responsibilities. I have noticed that most younger women already have this expectation of future partners (although they might add the question, "How do you make your partner an equal partner *and* still appreciate that person as a long-term romantic partner?"). Regardless, your partner is someone you will lean on heavily as you manage your career and your personal life. Being able to share in household responsibilities or child care is key if you want to maintain your sanity. If you don't yet have children, this is an important discussion to have with your partner. What are your expectations in terms of your partner's participation in caring for kids and domestic chores? What is your partner's expectation? Where will you use extra help, like cleaners or nannies, to free up both your schedules? Will you both keep working?

A note about flexibility: I realize that this is not possible for all people, especially those in lower-paying, hourly jobs. People in high-paying executive jobs might have many demands on their time, but they typically have more resources and flexibility to help them deal with those demands. Regardless of the socioeconomic level associated with a position, some professions just don't allow for flextime or working from home. Again, you need to assess your priorities. Which profession is going to meet first your financial needs and then your personal goals?

Putting It All Together

So many people despair over the lack of time in their lives. If they could only sleep less, commute less, or spend less time cleaning the house, then they could get that one last thing done. I don't share this resentment. Time is the great equalizer: we all, whether we work in an ice cream shop or are president of the United States, have equal amounts of it. The key to unlocking your time is the way you manage it.

Don't get discouraged by counting the hours you are working today, especially if you are at the start of your career. Recognize that priorities and work demands ebb and flow over months and years. The best thing you can do is take the time to thoughtfully plan a schedule that won't create resentment. Acknowledge that you are making choices about where you spend your time, whether that's work or home. If you're not happy with those choices, make different ones—but don't be blind to the trade-offs. The more you can get into the habit of feeling like your schedule is something you have thoughtfully created, the more you will feel like you are accomplishing all the things you want to be doing. In other words, having it all.

CHAPTER 4

Everything Speaks: Personal Brand Matters

I spend a lot of time reading about professional development and how to build better workplaces. My friends and colleagues know this and love to send me articles I think will be interesting. One day an article titled "Why We Respond Emotionally to Numbers" popped into my inbox.[1] I couldn't figure out why the friend who sent it thought I would be interested, but I started reading and quickly became captivated.

The gist of the article was that numbers—which appear to be the epitome of cold, quantitative thought—actually create emotional responses in us. One example mentioned is a study by researchers at Northwestern University that found we subconsciously gender numbers. Odd numbers are masculine, even are female. This isn't just a fun fact to pull out at a dinner party, though—the significance we assign numbers has real-world business application. A company that consults on the proper way to use numbers in branding explains that the number ten is an important number in business branding because we associate it with a sense of completion (perhaps because of our ten fingers—back when our mathematical abilities were less developed, ten of anything was the most we could easily count). Ten is an emotionally stable number; it connotes practicality and efficiency.

So what's the point here, why am I babbling about numbers and their impact beyond the mathematical? Because while reading this article I realized just how much *everything* about the way we present ourselves says something about us to the outside world. Whether it is fair or not (and it often isn't), we judge people by the way they present themselves. In the context of business, this idea has mainly been confined to discussions of how to dress or speak. This is a reductive view. The way you dress and speak does matter, but many other things matter also: what your business cards look like, how you've structured your Twitter handle, and what numbers you use in your marketing campaigns. *Everything speaks*, so make sure you know what you want to say and what you want to achieve with the message.

Technology has complicated personal branding. Before we were responsible for both our tangible and digital lives, it was much easier to control the message of our personal brand. How your personal brand translated in direct interactions was up to you, while the ways in which people interacted with your personal brand indirectly were limited to channels like books you wrote, your business materials, and PR. You had some control over most of these things. But now, as we discussed with regard to time management, there is very little separation between your personal and public spheres. We live in a world of work–life integration, and this applies to your personal brand as well. It's not enough to wear a perfectly tailored suit to work; you need to be presentable outside work too. It's not enough to have a squeaky clean LinkedIn profile; your Facebook or Twitter accounts also matter. Because of the overlap that integrating our work and personal lives has created, you have to have an *authentic* and *consistent* message running through all channels.

Notice those two words: authentic and consistent. This chapter is about how to create a personal brand that promotes you in your career; it is not about how to create a false impression of who you are, even if you think the "fake you" will sell better. As you begin to think about the kind of personal brand you want, it is tempting to embellish some of your abilities or interests to create what you think will be a more appealing version of you. Do not do this. Unless you are very skilled at manipulation, people will know when you are affecting an identity. Maybe not everyone all the time, but the experts and leaders in your field—those it's most important to impress—will have the experience to spot an actor a mile away. You don't have to market your complete self; there is an aspect of picking and choosing when it comes to your personal brand. But keep the brand authentic to you. If you choose to make your personal brand aspirational, make sure you can live up to it.

Your personal brand also needs to be consistent. I cannot stress this enough. As I said earlier, new digital technologies have allowed people unprecedented access to each other's personal lives. Content you post to social media should be congruent with the way you conduct yourself in meetings and the physical materials you distribute. Interviews you do should be in line with the message of your personal brand. That goes for blog posts, too. Any content by or about you needs to tie into the larger message of what you are trying to sell. In creating a personal brand, your job is to *craft a story that you can apply across channels to market your best self.* If one piece of content is off brand, people may start to question the credibility of your brand. This chapter is designed to help you be thoughtful about what you are sharing and why.

What Your Personal Brand Is Not: An Elevator Pitch

Besides "mentor," I would like to nominate "elevator pitch" as another candidate in the category of overused buzzwords (or, technically, buzz phrases). An elevator pitch is a thirty-second summation of something, usually a business, product, service, new venture—or you. The name is a clever way to explain that you need to be able to explain whatever it is you are pitching in the duration of a short elevator ride. In other words, brevity is key.

I used to hear the phrase "elevator pitch" most often in regard to investment pitches. Could a start-up team looking for funding explain their new venture in thirty seconds to prove that they had distilled the core concept of their business? Recently, the elevator pitch has been applied to personal brands. Can you explain who you are and what you do in thirty seconds or less? This ability was supposedly useful at networking events or during interviews, when you were going to need to explain yourself very quickly as you looked to either make connections or impress an interviewer. Having been on the receiving end of many a personal elevator pitch, I can tell you that it is both ineffective and outdated.

First, elevator pitches were popular for explaining new businesses, products, or services because they distilled the core competency of the offering. You should know your strengths and be able to communicate them, but humans are more complex than their core competencies. An elevator pitch is too narrow a platform to sell who you are and why people should be interested in you. Second, the utilitarian nature of an elevator pitch makes it awfully dry. Being barraged with the finer points of someone's résumé is unpleasant and generally does not give me a good sense of who the person is—or why I should care. It comes off as robotic and socially ungraceful—not attributes you want ascribed to you.

Instead of an elevator pitch, I believe that you must *tell a story* with your personal brand. People hate being doused with fact sheets, but they love stories. Who are you? What are you passionate about? How do your skills and passion tie into your career? What goals are you building toward? How did you get where you are? The key is building a narrative around your career journey that draws people in. When you are able to shape that journey into a story, you will aid people in fitting together the pieces. Why did you take six months off to travel in rural China? Because you have an expressed interest in the evolving local elections in Chinese villages. A firsthand perspective on nascent democratic practices informs your career as a political consultant now. That is also why you are studying Arabic. The pieces should all tie together. Your narrative should change over time as you refine your vision.

The way you deliver your story differs from the way you'd deliver an elevator pitch as well. An elevator pitch is about two lines of uninterrupted prose. A story is a dialogue.

Have the theme and plot points prepared, but the delivery will change based on the audience. This allows you to see which parts hook your listener and to develop those more deeply. Plus, people prefer conversations to lectures. The benefit of a conversation is that the listener is allowed to contribute. Certain aspects of your story might resonate with your listener. Perhaps the person you are speaking with has also been to China or is interested in the theories of democratic development. Giving your listener an in gives her a chance to offer information about herself. If you are hoping to strike up anything beyond a superficial exchange, the other person's participation is essential.

It is not an easy task to tell your story in a professionally convincing manner. Your story is not something you think up one day in the shower. It requires knowing what you are good at, what you do (a surprisingly challenging question for some people), what you want to do, and how all the pieces tie together. Try telling yourself your story—make yourself the hero (albeit a humble hero). What is your mission? Who are the supporting characters and how do they fit in? How do you explain divergences in the plot? What other skills do you need to amass to reach your goals? And most of all, does the picture you present of yourself match the story you want to tell?

Your personal brand should consistently support and tell your professional story—your brand is the best way for people to understand you without you actually having to tell them. The best part is that it is highly scalable, given the ways you can now promote yourself on digital channels. So how do you go about creating and promoting your personal brand?

First, you have to know what you are promoting—and to what end. As we have established, your brand cannot be inauthentic, but it should be a selection of the best pieces of what you want to communicate about yourself. Your message and the latitude you have with it will evolve as you grow in your career. At the moment, your personal brand might be as simple as "recent college graduate passionate about aviation with a range of technical skills." Later, it might become "aerospace and defense senior engineer with expertise in radar systems."

Step one is taking stock of what you already know: your core competencies and career goals. We have already talked about the importance of identifying your skill set and goals. Use those as the foundation for your personal brand. How you market that mix of abilities and ambition—your personal brand—can be broken down into two categories: your physical presentation and your digital presentation. I am using the phrase "physical presentation" broadly here to mean the following: your dress, hygiene, physical fitness, speech, and other small factors that relate to the way you present yourself in everyday life. People will read meaning into seemingly insignificant details, so you will need to develop a well-considered and thorough approach to your personal brand's expression. Your digital presentation is just what it sounds like: the impression you create on social media channels, blogs, and personal websites. It encompasses everything on the Internet by or about you. The rest of this chapter is about how to utilize every one of these channels. Remember: your strategies in these arenas will be different, but the message should be consistent.

Physical Presentation

Talking about your physical presentation—how you look, sound, and act—can be difficult. There is only so much we can change about who we are before we are either presenting an inauthentic version of ourselves or pushing the boundaries of our pocketbooks or natural gifts. You might have come across the term "executive presence." Executive presence refers to an amalgamation of traits that inspires people to follow you or promote you. The old model of executive presence advocated for tall, handsome men with a firm handshake, full of charisma, or attractive women in power suits walking a fine line between being nice and being assertive. Research shows that being tall and attractive does help your case, but don't despair if you are neither. The qualities we ascribe to people worthy of being followed—the people with executive presence—have expanded to encompass other attributes and styles of leadership.

This means that your aesthetic presentation does not have to be limited by your height, your wardrobe budget, or the kind of car you drive. In many professional settings today you don't even need a suit—and you definitely don't need a Tesla. Your personal brand might be about you as a programmer interested in applying your technical expertise to product development. What does this mean for the way you dress? The way you speak? What kinds of skills do you need to have, and what publications should you read? All the pieces tie in. Your brand is as much about creating congruency as it is about cutting out the incongruous bits. So if you are a programmer, as in our example above, and you wear a suit to your office in San Francisco every day while everyone else is rocking their startup tees, it's time to change tactics. Developers tend to dress very casually and are a little judgmental of techies who dress like VCs, just like if you were an investment banker who wore jeans to work in your Manhattan office you might get in trouble. The difference is that the Silicon Valley dress code is implicit, but you still want to adopt the right "uniform."

The breadth of attributes you need to consider when creating your personal brand is not limited to your dress. Because *everything* speaks, we can't cover here all the aspects you need to consider. Also, your perception of yourself and others' perception of you can be quite different. In your head—or, if you're like me, written down somewhere—is your plan for what your personal brand communicates about you. But how does this play out in real life? A useful way to think about your physical presentation is to ask yourself the following questions: When people look at me, what do they see? When I talk, what do they hear? Do these answers make sense relative to the message I am trying to send? Let's tackle these one at a time.

When People Look at Me, What Do They See?

Many negative things can be said about making superficial judgments (remember the old cliché, don't judge a book by its cover?), but the fact is, we all do it. Like it or not, your looks will be judged by others, including things as small as whether your nail polish is chipped.

We'll start with something basic and yet fundamental:

hygiene. You would be surprised by how many careers have been sidetracked by body odor or bad breath. There is no excuse here. Keep yourself smelling fresh, no matter how many all-nighters you pull. The more superficial aspects of your grooming—your hairstyle, for example—aren't governed by hard-and-fast rules. Look at your stated personal brand for cues. If you are a young man who's an investment banking analyst, you probably need to shave every day and have a shorter haircut, but if you work in digital marketing in Los Angeles, you probably don't. Women who work in fashion will have a different set of rules for the colors they can dye their hair than women who work in management consulting.

Clothing is a big issue, and is often mystifying for young people just beginning their careers. In this respect, men have it much easier than women. If men are required to wear professional clothing to work, several pairs of slacks, a few dress shirts, and a suit or two will take care of their wardrobe requirements. Ties are the hardest part. Women have it rough whether they work in an office that has strict dress requirements or one that allows casual attire. They have to be careful not to look too young, too old, too sexy, too conservative, or too eccentric. A wardrobe that is versatile but also affordable can be difficult to put together. My advice remains the same: think about what you are trying to communicate. Just because you are a woman in finance does not mean you have to wear a power suit (although you can if you want to and it makes sense). Consider well-tailored dresses and blazers with a conservative pair of heels or flats. A job that emphasizes creativity probably has a little more leeway for bright colors or trendy clothing. Or, if you work in a technical function, you might wear jeans and start-up-branded t-shirts that you snagged at a career fair. That's totally fine, as long as it's in line with the image you want to present. If you are completely lost, look at the way the more senior women and men in your office or industry dress. Learning by example is a fine way to go about it.

Your personal style should evolve with your personal brand. This might be surprising, but you actually have more flexibility with what you wear as you grow older. When you are younger and still establishing yourself, you will likely find yourself playing to certain expectations about entry-level analysts, consultants, engineers, and so on. Once you have a bit of success, the track record you have built buffers those expectations. For example, a local businessman in my town shows up to every meeting and event, no matter how formal, in jeans and cowboy boots. This is accepted because he is extremely successful and his style aligns with his "maverick" brand. But I would bet that he did not dress like that when he was beginning his career as a financial analyst at a big bank.

While it is fun to be creative and make waves, you do not *have* to take risks with your dress. Unless being a wild and crazy guy is integral to the brand you are trying to build, it is better to err on the side of tastefulness. If you choose to make a statement with your style, consider that statement well. There is a fine line to walk when being memorable for your style; you don't want to be known *just* for what you wear and not what you do. It is perfectly acceptable to have a professional wardrobe full of black dresses and nice sweaters and to get attention for your work instead. A safe way to test the waters on expanding your aesthetic brand is to develop a "signature item." Think of former Secretary of State Madeleine

Albright and her collection of pins, which brightened up many a dreary suit, or head of the IMF Christine Lagarde and her beautiful Hermès scarves. Don't be silly about it (i.e., don't be the girl who wears pink heels every day), but a small wardrobe statement that easily identifies you is a plus.

Your physical fitness is another important element of your physical presentation. You do not have to be in marathon shape, but research shows that being fit gives you several advantages in the workplace. First, I find that people tend to associate fitness with discipline and vitality. Research also shows that engaging in high-intensity exercise before a professional challenge—like an important presentation or a big meeting—actually helps you perform better in the meeting (thanks to those lovely little endorphins doing their job). So next time you're going to be in the spotlight, throw out those cram notes and grab your running shoes. Plus, it's just smart to take care of yourself.

You can overdo it on physical fitness, though. If you are a management consultant with the figure of a bodybuilder, the image doesn't necessarily make sense (unless you have a clever way to tie your physique into your "story"). People might wonder how and why you have the time to maintain those washboard abs—and whether that time might not be better spent developing less tangential professional goals.

Beware also that there is a difference between well-considered personal presentation and overly considered personal presentation. Men, especially, can get dinged for looking like they have spent too much time on their grooming (i.e., fit the metrosexual label). You want to look like you care, but not like you are self-obsessed and narcissistic. Both men and women need to be careful about excessive self-tanner or makeup. The same goes for expensive accessories. My rule is that it is a bad idea to have more expensive shoes than your boss, even if it means telling your mom to return those Gucci loafers she got you for Christmas. Designer clothing or hand-bags are not forbidden, but it does look a little suspicious when someone working an entry-level job is decked out in clothes worth thousands of dollars. Of course, it is no one's business how you afford what you have, but that doesn't mean they won't wonder.

Realize that your personal presentation isn't just about your grooming and clothes. What kind of car do you drive? What phone, computer, or tablet do you own? How have you decorated your office? Remember—*everything matters*. We are judged on the total package. So do a little exercise and con-sider all the things that are an extension of you, and assess whether they are "on brand." If you work as a financial con-troller and want to be known as a thrifty guy, don't drive a luxury sports car. If you are a lobbyist for an environmental firm, you probably shouldn't drive a luxury sports car either (there are lovely alternative energy options for you). Don't work hard on your looks, only to forget that everyone will notice you are still using a flip phone. From start to finish, people's perceptions of you must make sense with what you are selling. Our integrated lives demand consistency in all forums.

A final note of caution: as you consider your presen-tation, you have to think about how *all* people see you, not just how people your age see you. Some aspects of personal presentation are generational. For example, visible tattoos are much more accepted by millennials than they are by the generations that preceded them. If you work in a casual environment with people your age, maybe that inspirational script behind your ear is fine. But if there is any chance your older boss might react negatively to it, perhaps hold off—or get the tattoo in a place that can be easily concealed. I am not telling you to curb self-expression, but to be realistic about the aspects of your presentation that might have a negative effect on your career, fair or not.

When I Speak, What Do People Think?

As we will see in chapter 5, one of the fundamental Four Cs is *communication*. If you can't get your point across or carry on a conversation, your on-point appearance won't matter.

Much of our verbal presentation has to do with the way we talk. Is your voice deep or very high? Do you have any verbal tics or a noticeable regional accent? This is another area in which women tend to have more trouble than men. Deep voices are seen as more authoritative. A high-voiced woman attempting to be assertive may be accused of being shrill. Or, if you get nervous, you might have a tendency to get squeaky. Sometimes, especially around a dinner table at a noisy restaurant, high voices are just harder to hear. Work on moderating your voice so that you aren't always speaking in your upper register. There are vocal coaches who can help if you sense this is a problem for you. Some people only have this issue when they are talking on the phone. I know women who have worked on developing a "phone voice" so they sound less girlish when making calls.

Apart from vocal register, there are plenty of common verbal mistakes people make when they are speaking in a professional capacity. The biggest one is talking too quickly. Unless you are a race announcer or a floor trader, you do not need to be a motormouth (I tried and failed to picture a professional personal brand that incorporated this style of speech). How loudly or softly do you talk? Even your diction matters, especially the way you vary it depending on circumstances. You want to speak one way while giving a speech at your company's annual shareholders' meeting and another at the lunch table with the people on your team.

Does the Image I Project Make Sense for My Brand?

Ask yourself whether the image you've put together aligns well with your personal brand. Review your image frequently. Ask friends you can trust and maybe even a colleague who won't think you're being narcissistic. If you're terribly unsure, this is one scenario where I encourage you to hire an executive coach or marketing specialist. Our self-image can vary wildly from others' perceptions, both in negative and positive ways. So try to be honest with yourself and remember to build your personal brand in a way that reflects the best business version of you.

Digital Presentation

The evolving digital landscape has opened up countless meaningful opportunities to develop and capitalize on your personal brand. However, these new channels add a considerable amount of work. Which ones should you be using and how often? What kind of content do you need to create? Who will monitor the Internet for content about you or your company and make sure it is on brand? What is your intention in engaging with social media or writing a blog?

Before you jump into the digital sphere just because it seems like you should, you need to know what your objectives are. It is difficult to analyze ROI on digital engagement, so have an idea of reasonable goals for building your brand digitally. If you want to build an entire business out of your fashion blog and associated YouTube tutorials, you are going to look at different metrics than someone who occasionally posts to a personal blog of ruminations on industry developments. No matter what, creating a dynamic digital presence takes time—more time than people usually anticipate. Is the return worth it? The worst thing you can do is to engage intermittently on social media or your blog, if your intention is to have an active digital brand. If you decide that it isn't worth it to you to build out your digital brand, that's okay. Just make sure your contact information and an updated LinkedIn page are available so people can find you when they need to.

If you decide to have a digital personal brand, you have many channels available to you. The first way many people dipped a toe into digital branding was by creating personal websites and blogs. This is an easy way to start broadcasting yourself. As with your personal style, unless you have professional help or an eye for design, keep things simple. Your digital aesthetic should reflect your personality as much as your tangible style does. If you still aren't sure how to do it, say less rather than more. The same questions you ask yourself about your physical presentation can be easily adapted to your digital brand: What do people think when they look at my website/social media accounts? What do they think when they read/look at/watch what I have posted?

Social media, once considered important only for personal reasons, now has broad professional applications. In some industries it is now almost a requirement that you engage on at least one platform. On the Internet, as in real life, remember that we are now integrating rather than separating and balancing. You can keep distinct personal and professional social media accounts, but most people don't. It's cumbersome and less interesting than presenting a holistic picture of who you are. But, be smart about what you are choosing to post and where; for example, maybe hold back on posting that vacation bikini pic to Instagram unless you are an up-and-coming model and the photo has real brand value.

This means you also have to be vigilant about what people post about you. A well-meaning friend might put up a picture of a raucous Halloween party you attended in a skimpy catsuit. So before you put on that costume, consider whether pictures might make their way onto the Internet, and dress accordingly. Second, there's no shame in asking someone to take a picture down, provided you can explain gracefully why you are worried about it. Don't be a jerk and risk an angry ex-friend posting risqué content featuring you all over the Internet (if this happens, and it is an extreme case, there are legal means of dealing with it).

The most perplexing behavior I see, though, comes from the person who, while careful in his physical presentation, is apparently thoughtless when it comes to what he posts online. When I say everything speaks, that goes for your Twitter, Facebook, and Snapchat accounts, too. I can't tell if the drunken photos or insensitive rants are momentary lapses in judgment or show a complete disregard for the fact that anything put on the Internet is a permanent fixture that may be found by the public. Regardless, I think this phenomenon is worth discussing.

The Price of Forgetting Work–Life *Integration*

My favorite story of a person flagrantly disregarding the importance of aligning her physical and digital brands comes from my hometown of Calgary. In early 2015, a young Calgary politician named Deborah Drever won an upset election for the Legislative Assembly of Alberta, a huge boon for the twenty-six-year-old and a testament to her charisma. However, right after she was elected, controversy erupted. On her social media accounts Drever had posted images that showed her endorsing illegal drug use and flipping off the flag of Canada. Not a good branding move for a budding politician. As reporters (and the public) delved further, the situation only got worse, with Drever's images and statements seeming to support everything from sexual assault to homophobia. It took only a few days of public uproar for her to be suspended from her political party.[2] Her glory was short-lived and totally tainted by the negative press.

The kind of ill-advised behavior politician Deborah Drever exhibited in her social media use is mind-boggling to me (see sidebar). She had worked so hard to win an election—how could she not have realized that the racy and intolerant content she was posting would be career defining? And that's where the answer was, I realized. She just wasn't thinking. Nor are most people when they post questionable things online. I wish I could say this is a problem exclusive to the young, but it isn't. How many high-powered politicians and executives have accidentally posted private and intimate pictures in a way that ultimately cost them their career?

If you post something on the Internet, even if you have privacy controls set up, people can find it. You have to be thoughtful—almost paranoid—about only posting content that is appropriate and makes sense with the image you want associated with you. Remember that anything you put on the Internet is permanent, even if it doesn't feel that way. Just because you delete a picture you posted on one of your social media accounts doesn't mean it hasn't been saved as a screen-shot or archived. Plus, most tech companies back up all digital media anyway, so beware of apps offering "disappearing" communications. In an age of hackers, investigations, and people just being spiteful, remember that nothing is private, not even your personal e-mail. Hopefully, you are considerate about how you use your work e-mail, but this caution applies to your personal e-mail as well. Thoughtless messages sent to your fraternity listserv in college can come back to haunt you.

The Internet is a powerful tool, but it's often used carelessly. Establish your digital presence with a strong plan and be committed to maintaining what you start. Make sure your messaging is consistent across all channels, and that the story you tell in your real life matches what you live online. The power of the Internet lies in how many people you can reach without having to interact with them directly. Plus, you can't hire someone to give your speeches for you but you can hire

someone to run your Twitter account. Take advantage of digital content outsourcing as it makes sense for your business
and brand.

Putting It All Together

A well-considered personal brand is pivotal to growing your
career. Authenticity and consistency are the keystones on
which your brand will be built. There is one more element,
though, that I would like to address as I wrap up this chapter:
all your personal brand building will be meaningless if people don't like the image you are presenting to them. Notice I
am not saying that your personal brand has to be *likable*. Steve
Jobs, for example, was thought to be a tyrant and a narcissist.
It didn't matter, though, because the public sentiment around
his genius and the cool products he created was so strong. He
wasn't likable, but people liked what he was selling.

The same goes for the personal brand you create. You
don't have to be likable (although it's the rare person who
gets away with this), but—as with Steve Jobs—people have
to want what you're selling. Your personal brand might
not be about being "nice"—you might be assertive and
demanding—but the qualities you display have to be effective and congruent with your branded leadership style. Figure out what makes people want to follow you or listen to
you, and use that as a guiding point for your personal brand.
Your personal brand won't matter if no one is inspired by the
story you are telling.

CHAPTER 5

The Four Cs You Won't Learn in B-School

No matter what education people have been given, they are rarely taught the four foundational elements that will make all the difference in their careers: confidence, communication, commitment, and competence. These are attributes I see in every one of the high-achieving people I have worked with in my career.

The first is *confidence*, or your ability to act with conviction. The second, *communication*, is your ability to authentically connect with others and make yourself heard. The third attribute is *commitment*, or your ability to connect with the mission of your company outside of your own ego. And the final C is the least flashy but the most important: *competence*, or your ability to do your job.

The First C: Confidence

Confidence is a key determinant of success in the workplace. But, I believe we view confidence very narrowly. We often discuss confidence as an intrinsic quality—you have it or you don't—and we assume the more confidence one has, the better. Neither is true. Confidence can be built through experience and risk-taking. In addition, while having too little confidence is an issue, having too much is problematic as well.

The importance and complexities of confidence are explored brilliantly in Katty Kay and Claire Shipman's book *The Confidence Code*. The book examines confidence with the intent of figuring out how and why women are seemingly less confident than men, and why this holds women back in the workforce. First it is important to define confidence, which is also trickier than you might expect. My natural inclination, when I think about someone who is confident, is to ascribe adjectives like "domineering," "assertive," and maybe even "aggressive"—I think of the alpha males of the world. Kay and Shipman had a similar predisposition. After conversations with sociologists, psychologists, and prominent leaders, they arrive at an unexpected definition: confidence is the ability to act. Confident people insert themselves into the conversation, start businesses, and make decisions. Insecure people are paralyzed by their anxieties and fears. As they continued their research, Kay and Shipman discovered a "confidence gap" between men and women, particularly in the workplace. Men speak up in meetings, volunteer to give presentations, and apply for positions they're not qualified for. Women consider their words, allow opportunities to go to others, and only apply when they meet 100 percent of the criteria. In other words, they do not act.

I was not surprised to read these findings in *The Confidence Code*. In addition to my years working in human resources, I am also a platform partner of the Lean In Foundation. Several years ago, we ran the first Lean In Circles in major cities. Participants in the Circles were high-powered, successful young women who wanted to take advantage of the wisdom of a group of like-minded peers. As we sat in our Circle and the young women began to share some of the issues they confronted at work, I was shocked that most of them were plagued with self-doubt over their effectiveness at work. If any women should be insulated from this kind of self-recrimination, it was this group. It was eye-opening to see that a lack of confidence is not accompanied by a lack of ability or talent. These women were accomplished and qualified. But your talents don't matter if you never have the courage to apply them.

Fortunately, Kay and Shipman do not end their book on a dark note of science proving that generally women are in fact less confident than men. Instead, Kay and Shipman seek to discover whether confidence is innate or learned. As it turns out, it's a bit of both. We are born with certain genetic selectors that more or less predispose us to higher levels of confidence, but our parents, environment, and the way we treat ourselves have an even greater effect on our confidence. In other words, we can actively choose to build confidence for ourselves.

How does one go about building confidence? By constantly pushing our own limits into "risky" endeavors, by testing our abilities and seeing how far we get. Confidence is not about getting that one big promotion and feeling great about yourself, it is about the longer journey made up of many small failures and many small wins. You can create these opportunities for yourself. For example, if you are terrified of public speaking, do not immediately sign yourself up to speak at an event with five hundred attendees. Instead, start by giving speeches in your home alone, imagining an audience in front of you. Then create a real audience out of a few close friends. Take a public speaking class where the instructor requires active participation. *Then* volunteer yourself to be one of your company's speakers at the next customer appreciation event. By the time you are speaking in front of hundreds, you will have a track record of success that you can draw from.

I believe the best way to instill confidence is to first figure out where your abilities (or core competencies) are, and then slowly raise the bar for yourself—but never to the extent that you are not sure that you can do it. You should absolutely take risks, but do not set yourself up for failure. Notice that I am not saying, "Don't fail"—that would be silly. Failure is an inevitable part of taking risks, but fail small and fail fast. You will learn as much from your mistakes as you do from your successes. And a great part of confidence is that when we believe in our choices, we rarely regret them. Even the ones that did not turn out well have something to teach us.

Instead of waiting for opportunities to build your confidence, make confidence building an intentional part of your day. You can do this both actively and reactively. Actively pursue confidence by setting yourself one challenge a day—something that pushes you out of your comfort zone—and executing on it. Maybe you want to send a networking e-mail to a role model who both inspires and intimidates you. Perhaps you have a weekly product meeting that you rarely speak up in. It could even be a step toward a larger goal (i.e., you could sign yourself up for a class in a field that you think might offer a better career for you). Whatever the particulars are, the more opportunities you have to build confidence, the more confidence you will gain. You become comfortable with making assessments, making choices, and sticking with them. If you want to be really serious about it, keep a log of the challenges you present yourself with and track your progress. Looking back on that list of accomplishments should be enough to make you feel proud.

Practicing confidence reactively involves taking action when you are confronted with negative attitudes in yourself and others. We all have the tendency to criticize ourselves. Instead of continuing down these negative wormholes, stop yourself. Figure out *why* you are being so tough on yourself, or even take a moment to consider the criticism—and then move on. Kay and Shipman devote an entire chapter to healthier methods of self-talk, from not taking things so personally to killing negative thoughts (surprise: men once again are better at this than women—they do not dwell on their perceived shortcomings quite so much). It all comes down to your ability to have perspective and to be calm. An article I read recently put it well: "Confidence isn't arrogance, it's based on a constant awareness of how short life is and how little we ultimately lose from risking everything."[1] The next time you get nervous about raising your hand in a meeting, ask yourself what you are really risking by speaking up.

One more note before moving on to our second C: at the

beginning of this section I mentioned overconfidence. Studies have shown that this is a masculine trait—and that it has many positive effects in the business world. Tilting slightly toward overconfidence can win you promotions, the admiration of your peers, and the trust of your managers (even if it makes problems for you in the long run).[2] People like confident people. But, as Kay and Shipman say, even a popular pilot has to be able to land an airplane. In other words, your competence matters. In addition, while it is good to be a little overconfident, you can take it too far. This happens most frequently when people adhere to the traditional definition of confidence: pushy, assertive, dominant. It is not only men who make this mistake; I have observed women trying to adopt more "masculine" definitions of confidence in order to be powerful. Don't confuse throwing your weight around with being confident. Confidence is authentically pursuing what you believe is the right choice—and the way you message that choice makes all the difference.

The Second C: Communication

There are many styles of effective communication, so what I want to underscore is that communication is fundamental to every business interaction. Most corporate crises could have been averted with better communication, either internal or external. Think about CEO Tony Hayward's lack of response during the BP oil spill and how that exponentially compounded an already toxic situation. Or consider the inappropriate reply of former Lululemon chairman Chip Wilson, who responded to a quality issue with the company's yoga pants by saying that the product wasn't designed to fit some women's bodies.[3] Communication is a must, but bad communication can turn a mistake into a crisis.

Because having your message understood is so critical, I believe that frequent communication is better than minimal communication. If anything, you want to err on the side of overcommunication. Update your manager or client on your progress more often than you think is necessary; they will tell you if it is too much. You also can't assume that your point has been understood, even if you feel that you have been clear (this may not be an issue for project updates, but is certainly a possibility when you are trying to agree on project strategies and goals). Find low-impact ways to ensure that the recipient has understood your message, even if this means sending bulleted e-mails with the agreed-upon points and asking for a simple "yes" or "no" response.

How do you apply your communications skills appropriately across all channels? In the workplaces of yesteryear, you had to be able to communicate in person and perhaps by telephone (landline, not cell) or letter. Now, technology has enabled manifold and constant communication streams with our coworkers and clients. My phone is both my best and worst tool. Effective communication today comes with two challenges: first, managing all of your communication channels, and second, creating the correct boundaries and expectations.

Let's begin with a discussion of communication channels. What are the different methods of communication you use at work? It would not be unusual if you e-mailed, called, texted, instant-messaged, videoconferenced, and held in-person meetings. On top of that, maybe your team uses a project management tool like a calendar or digital to-do list that is collaborative. Maybe you even tweet at each other. That's a lot to stay on top of, considering that each mode of communication has both its benefits and pitfalls.

E-mail

E-mail is the mode of communication that gets the most attention in business books and advice columns today. I can understand why. If you are not careful, your inbox can overflow with thousands of e-mails, and important things get lost in the deluge. Many people could spend their entire day answering e-mails, as we discussed in the section detailing time management. If you have control over your e-mail schedule, plan to check e-mail only a few times a day, and keep messages you send as short and clear as possible.

Videoconferencing

While calling on the phone is still the go-to method, I find more and more people these days are offering videoconferencing as an alternative. I like this, considering that it can be a cost-effective alternative to long-distance international conference calls. However, the same rules that you would follow for in-person meetings apply. Be presentable, make eye contact, and be sure to hold your videoconference in a quiet place (how many times do you see people holding business Skype calls from Starbucks?). Test the speed of your Internet connectivity before agreeing to the call, and if your connection is bad, do a regular voice call instead.

Texts, Instant Messages, and Group Chats

Instant messaging and texting are the most informal methods of communication that are currently integrated into the workplace. The informal nature of these communications doesn't mean that you can be unprofessional while using them, however—this is the biggest mistake I see people make. Whether employees are using the instant messaging service for office gossip or are neglecting spelling in texts, they seem to forget that these are work-related conversations. Be aware of how you are representing yourself and the company. But don't overdo it either—for example, there's no need to begin texts with "Dear So-and-so" (that will date you quickly).

You want to be careful, too, because the brevity of texts and IMs makes them easy to misinterpret. Be sure your messages don't leave room for interpretation and, if you are afraid the intent might be lost, choose a different form of communication. Pick up the phone or go find the person you need to talk to. It should go without saying that sensitive conversations should not be conducted over text or IM (that's the stuff of middle school romances).

Also, remember that if a conversation is conducted on a work device, or even using a personal device at work, your company owns that conversation. I have seen some pretty interesting things unearthed in people's IM history, Internet search history, and e-mail archives. Don't send anything that you wouldn't want your boss or HR department to know about.

With so many different methods of communication

available at all times, how do you manage them effectively? I believe the best way is to first find out your manager's, clients', or coworkers' expectations of your availability. For example, do you work at a company that expects you to answer e-mails after work hours? Do you need to check your work phone on weekends? How quickly does your boss expect you to respond to her e-mails? Is an hour lag okay, or does she want an immediate response? There may be no hard-and-fast rules, but it is best to find out what the unspoken expectations are. Every company evolves its own culture of communication. Whether or not you agree with the rules, you need to understand the norms for communication within your company.

Once you know what is expected of you, you should establish your own boundaries or rules for your communication channels. Figure out the expectations for response times, and then create corresponding windows for yourself to check e-mail or, as we discussed in the time management chapter, set others' expectations about how often you will be responding to your e-mail (if you have this power). Maybe you will check in three times a day, or maybe you'll do it the last ten minutes of every hour.

Insulate yourself from your bad habits. As tempting as it is to sleep with your phone next to your pillow, don't do it. About an hour before you go to sleep, put your phone away. Give your brain some time to relax without staring at an LCD screen. As long as you establish expectations about when and how you will be available, you shouldn't run into trouble. The trouble starts when people either don't understand what is expected from them (i.e., that they do, in fact, need to be available by e-mail over the weekend) or when they don't set up any boundaries and find themselves attending to work 24–7 on a multitude of devices.

The Third C: Commitment

Unfortunately, the speed with which you respond to an off-hours work e-mail or text is sometimes used as a proxy for your commitment to your job. But our third C, *commitment*, is about something much deeper than being on your phone constantly. Anyone can work long hours, but are you the kind of employee who understands the broader mission of your company, and is not always acting in his own self-interest? Commitment means being all in, being excited about becoming part of something larger than yourself.

This is a book about you and your career, about how to make yourself successful and fulfilled in your work. But there is a difference between self-reflection and self-focus. Even if you are competent, confident, and a great communicator, you will doom yourself if you are also an arrogant, self-involved shyster. If all your efforts are for your own advancement, it will show. The danger in investing time in employees who are motivated only by self-gain is that they may leave at the drop of a hat, showing no loyalty to the company that helped them grow. You do not owe everything to the company that employs you—but the company *does* pay you, and being committed to its mission makes for a happier partnership. Know when to push for a promotion or raise, but also know when to let your personal needs take a backseat to the team. There's even an element of being strategically selfish: if you grab every opportunity that comes up, you won't have a chance to be seen as a manager of other people. The point of being a manager is to delegate effectively and help others shine. If you're constantly taking the attention and credit for yourself, you can't do this. In today's cutthroat talent markets, commitment is what will set you apart.

There is a secret in the battle to be your company's most dedicated worker. I want to be careful about how I position the following advice, because taken the wrong way the practice could be very damaging: sometimes it is not how hard you work but the perception of how hard you work that matters. Recently, I listened to an excellent *Harvard Business Review* podcast that discussed the idea that at times it is the *perception* of how committed we are rather than how hard we are actually working that matters.[4] In other words, Person A and Person B are both executing on all their deliverables, and both are thought to be very hard workers. Person A shows up at the office at 6:30 a.m. every day and leaves well after dark, and she works while at home and takes calls during the weekend. Person B, however, takes calls from his kid's soccer practice, varies his hours, and takes meetings out of the office on Fridays so he can get home at a reasonable time. Person B is not less committed, he is just more strategic about how he uses his time. Person B delivers great work, and the impression of his coworkers is that he is putting in just as much effort as Person A, though he is not pulling the hundred-hour weeks Person A does. If you are getting your work done and are being respectful of the expectations of your company, I think Person B's approach is perfectly acceptable. My only note of caution is that I wouldn't go around bragging about how smart you are to have created this perception of yourself.

The last thing you want is a whole group of resentful people coming after you.

While you don't have to subscribe to our current cultural obsession with busyness, you should be passionate about or invested in your company. When you take that entry-level analyst job at a Fortune 500 company or that director position at a start-up of ten people, make sure you are all in—and in it for the right reasons. It will be better for the company if you have this attitude because you will not always be focusing on your own needs. It will be better for you, too; work is more fun and more fulfilling when you are engaged in and passionate about what you do. One real-world example that I love is about a team at Yahoo that named itself "Moneyball."[5] This group of eighteen people was given the task of revamping Yahoo's native ad functionality. Working crazy hours together, they pulled off their task in just over one month. This is the kind of dedication you want to see from a team—and reward if you are a manager. CEO Marissa Mayer apparently agrees, and sent the entire team to Hawaii as a thank-you.

The Fourth C: Competence

Much of the advice about getting ahead in the workplace is related to things like being a good public speaker, networking effectively, or keeping up a great social media presence. Don't get me wrong, these elements—along with many others—are important if you are going to take control of your career; all of the Four Cs are important. But one foundational element is often left out of the equation because it's a little more obvious and a little less sexy than a topic like executive presence. I am talking about *competence*, the ability to be good at the day-to-day mechanics of your job. Without this, nothing else matters.

There is an argument to be made that being a great pretender or having enough grit (a new buzzword—I have a whole shelf devoted to books on grit) is enough to make you succeed in business. Everyone knows that guy who's amazing at making himself sound like the most important, well-connected person on the planet. He might have talked himself into an impressive job or even an accelerated series of promotions (ever heard of the Peter Principle, aka being "promoted to your own level of incompetence"?).[6] But eventually, he will be asked to manage a team, write a proposal, or build a cost model—stuff he's bragged about doing but clearly never done—and it will all fall apart. Faking it can take you far, but eventually you hit the reality wall. The same goes for people who think that if they just work hard enough they will succeed. Again, being a hard worker is critical to success, but you need more than hard work. You need to be strategic about your goals, you need to understand your skill set, and you need to apply that skill set to getting the right things done.

Unfortunately, so many people are so focused on building their bright future that they forget to assess whether they have the tools to succeed in the present. You can dream big dreams and feel like you are killing yourself to make them happen, but are you doing your actual day-to-day job well? I see this problem crop up most often in ambitious young people. They are usually well educated and very invested in their career. They might even be a little bored by their analyst or entry-level engineering role. But in the midst of plotting their success, networking with the executive team, and building an app, they neglect the job their manager needs them to do on a daily basis. Please, don't forget to keep an eye on the tasks in your job description. If you do, it will come back to haunt you. This is not an uncommon mistake; I can't tell you how often I see it in my line of business.

I am focusing here on the younger age group because in my consulting work I constantly encounter driven young people who don't understand why they have been at their job a year and are not being promoted. They assume that their impressive degree and internships are enough to put them on the fast track. They came in with a head start, right? Here's the thing: they didn't. Getting a great degree and a variety of experiences as an intern is really, really important. But neither of those things will fully prepare you for working full time at a long-term job. Internships end after a few months, and college, which is meant to prepare you for your career, does so in a limited fashion.

I am not picking on liberal arts degrees here. Even those employees with technical degrees like computer science find that programming in a systems class and programming in the real world are not the same. (Just a note—the students typically best prepared for working life are those who have done a long-term work-study program during college.) It is great to read classical French or have a theoretical understanding of black holes, but will either of those things matter in your job as a financial analyst? Do your education and experiences translate into a working skill set for the job you want? It's okay if the answer is "no" or "partially." Remember, your education does not end with graduation. The key is to identify your gaps and then fill them.

So, how do you identify your weaknesses, the areas of your job where you are incompetent (or not as competent as you would like to be)? Start with your manager—but I do not recommend going to your manager and saying, "Tell me all the things I'm bad at." This is not a topic you want your manager to dwell on. Instead, try time-tested lines like, "Where do you see areas for improvement?" or "What kind of skills would your ideal candidate bring to this role?" The last one you can even ask in interviews. Another way to handle this is to ask your manager what kind of skills a person the level up from you would have. If it's better SQL or fluency in Spanish, you can start working on that now. Then, when you go to make your business case for being promoted, you can detail all the qualifications you have that go with the job description for the next level.

Some people aren't eager to ask their managers about their areas for improvement, and I understand that—it's scary to be told where you might be falling short. But, one, you need to know what you're not great at if you want to improve and, two, generally managers won't hit you with anything too painful (trust me, if there were big problems you would already know). Managers are pleased when you show interest in mastering your daily tasks. I hear from many managers that their direct reports have room to improve in areas like Excel skills, PowerPoint presentations, and public speaking—and that is all achievable. I even find that companies are willing to sponsor their employees to take classes in areas directly related to their jobs. If you can go to your manager and thoughtfully argue why a class in Tableau will make you a more effective employee, I guarantee she will be impressed. You'll get big brownie points if you suggest bringing in an expert to help your whole work group develop a particular skill you all need (i.e., finding someone to do an Excel short course).

Aside from your manager, there are resources you can use to assess your skill set, especially if you are not aiming for a promotion but instead want to transfer industries or start your own business. If you get really motivated, you can find a career coach familiar with your industry to advise you. Mentors can also offer advice: What skills do they believe would be useful for you to develop at this point in your career? What skills do they wish they had worked on when they were your age? Do a self-check with your peer group as well. Do all the analysts around you have amazing Visual Basic skills? Then you probably should, too.

Do the following exercise, and be honest: think about your day from start to finish. What tasks do you routinely perform and what skills do you need to execute them perfectly? On a scale of one to ten, how would you rate yourself on each of those skills? If you are feeling brave, share the list with your manager and get his feedback as well. Stepping away from the mentor myth entails taking control of your career, so getting your manager involved may seem counterintuitive, but part of taking control is utilizing all the resources available to you. Your manager is a resource, as are your mentors and peers. You are taking control by actively seeking feedback instead of passively showing up to work day after day with no idea of the skill set you need to be building.

In talking about competence, I have been careful to keep the discussion focused on your current situation (are you good at what you do *now*?). That's because I often see people so fixed on moving forward that they forget about mastering their current job. They confuse working hard with working well. There is no mistaking this: you will not be promoted or you will not be able to start your own endeavor until you have all the skills necessary to do so. No skipping steps. But you don't want to neglect your future. You can lay a great foundation for that next step without detracting from your quest to achieve excellence in your current role. I've already mentioned asking your manager about the skills you need to move up. You should also take a look at your role models and figure out what they do really well—are you good at those things too? If the partner you admire at your firm writes great, concise investment briefs, then try to develop your ability to do so. Follow the examples of your role models. There's no need to reinvent the wheel.

A final note on competence: this section has focused mainly on assessing your skill set and plugging the holes you find. The other side of the coin is equally important—in what areas are you already really great? I learned this lesson the hard way. Early in my career I was on a road trip with my company's regional manager. We were headed from Vancouver to Seattle to attend a Seahawks game, and he had specifically asked if we could drive together so we could visit. The first question he asked me was, "What are you good at?" I could name every one of my weaknesses and I knew I was good at my job, but for the life of me I couldn't come up with anything concrete. He refused to change the subject, trying different angles and scenarios to help me think of an acceptable answer. I still cringe when I think about that drive; those three hours were the longest of my life, and are seared into my brain. When I got out of the car I vowed to always be able to articulate the assets I bring to the business.

What are your strengths, your key competencies? You want to know those things, too, so you can place yourself in roles that emphasize your abilities. When an interviewer asks how you add value, you can list those things. Maybe those are skills you want to put even *more* time into developing, because someday you'll hang your entire career on them. Figure out your weaknesses, but know your strengths.

Putting It All Together

In business school, or in your undergraduate degree, you might learn financial modeling skills, basic programming, or the right way to launch a digital marketing campaign. These are examples of useful skills, but just having those skills without the framework of the four Cs will seriously inhibit your career.

The four Cs provide the foundation on which your skillset can shine. Each is pivotal. You need to know what you are good at (competence). Then, you need to have faith in your abilities and decisions to execute on what you are good at (confidence). But that's not enough either—you need to be able to demonstrate your effectiveness and thinking to your coworkers so they recognize what you are good at, too (communication). And finally, you have to have the grit and determination to see your job through (commitment).

All four of these attributes will play an instrumental role in your professional journey. You might be weak in one attribute and strong in another. Take some time to diagnose how comfortable you feel with each of the Cs and then make a game plan for how you can build your proficiency. This chapter contains strategies for working on each independently, but it is the combination of the four that will propel you forward.

Be aware that your strength in each of the Cs will change depending on where you are in your career. Just because you achieve maximum competence in one role does not mean you have hit your career ceiling in competence—in other words, that you will never have to worry about being competent again. For example, you might be very confident in your current role, but if you are promoted to a different position with new responsibilities, you will need to work to build some of that confidence again. Similarly a new position at work will mean reevaluating how your core competencies apply to your new job. Your work with the four Cs is never done, so keep constant attention on improving your strength with each.

CHAPTER 6

Your Network and Sponsors

It is tempting to think that taking control of your career is a one-person show, but that is not the case. Your road to success depends on you proactively calling the shots while using all available resources. In this chapter, we will discuss how to create an effective network of mentors, sponsors, peer mentors, and role models. Notice that mentors are included in this list of resources, but I add them with a cautionary note: don't fall victim to the mentor myth—your mentors are here to augment your career, not be responsible for it. The same caution applies to peer mentors (people your own age whom you respect and trust), sponsors (people who not only give you advice but promote your work), and role models.

Your network is a key part of your professional success. But building a network is not an intuitive skill for most people. It is also an iterative process; you are never finished, and the way you develop your network will change as you grow your own career. When you begin networking you are still figuring out your interests and career goals. Because of this, you must cast as large a net as possible among the people you can contact—family friends, school alumni, and more. By sorting among the contacts you make using this open-ocean approach, you will learn what careers appeal to you and the kinds of people who are most helpful. As you understand your ambitions better, you will become a better networker as well, able to quickly spot the diamond in the rough among your contacts.

The mistake most people—especially young people—make is that they get themselves stuck in the wide-net-casting approach to networking. They connect with random people on LinkedIn (I can't even count how many of these requests I get) or indiscriminately attend networking events in their area. They do not become more selective about choosing which people will be most helpful to them or which people they will be most helpful to. You can absolutely over-network and waste your time. Or you can choose the wrong targets and put lots of time into developing relationships that go nowhere. This chapter will discuss the key relationships you need to focus on when building your network: mentors, peer mentors, sponsors, and role models. I don't promote the traditional networking idea of "grabbing coffee" with as many high-level executives as you can; my advice here is about building strategic, long-term relationships that will become the pillars of your career.

But remember—there is a difference between relying on other people to help you get ahead and thinking your success depends on the influence of others. The difference is that you are in the driver's seat. You want someone to help you navigate but you don't want a backseat driver or, even worse, someone who will take over the wheel altogether.

Your network will help propel you, but your ultimate success depends on your efforts.

Mentors

I began this book by discussing the dangers of overemphasizing the importance of mentors. To recap: mentors are overutilized, undertrained, and routinely underdeliver. The current body of thought around mentorship suggests that mentors are an irreplaceable part of your professional journey and that mentorship is even capable of fixing industry-wide problems such as a lack of diversity. The message is: if you want to win, you have to have a mentor. And if you don't have one, you're in trouble.

What Mentors Can and Cannot Do for You

Mentors can be an effective tool, but they are not a silver bullet. A mentor *is* meant to be an experienced source of advice, someone with whom you have a close personal relationship and who gives you excellent professional feedback. If you can find such a person and establish a working partnership, that's wonderful. If you can't, your career is not lost.

You might be lucky enough to be part of a formal mentoring program that requires mentors to undergo training and keep a check-in schedule with you. If the training was adequate, if your mentor has time to keep the schedule, and if you and your mentor are compatible, then this is an excellent recipe for successful mentoring.

Unfortunately, most mentors are not trained in the specific skills a mentor needs to have. Relationships with mentors will differ, but all mentors must be able to listen, weigh priorities, see the big picture, and give thoughtful advice. They need to know the line between helping you think a decision through and empowering you to act on your own. They need to know the scope of their expertise and when something you're asking them is outside their knowledge base. They need to understand the time and personal connection a good mentor–mentee relationship requires.

By the evolving definition of mentorship, mentors are doomed to fail their mentees. Good advice is critically important, but no one can get it right 100 percent of the time. Mentors are human, too. They are subject to the same constraints of knowledge that you are. While their experience gives them a more developed perspective from which to advise you, they are not infallible. As I discussed earlier, mentors' advice can sometimes even be outdated. You might have a better understanding of developing technologies that will disrupt your industry than they do. Mentors might underdeliver, but this is partially because their utility is overemphasized. Furthermore, what works for one person doesn't always translate for another. This is one of the largest pitfalls of mentors: they draw on their personal experiences to give advice, but they are not you. Another person simply cannot understand all the nuances of your particular situation. Only you are the sum of your collective experiences, desires, and fears. So, the person best able to advise you is yourself.

On a broader scale, expectations for the impact of mentorship are wildly unrealistic. I agree that having mentors can help women and minorities make strides in industries where they are underrepresented—but mentorship will not have a material impact (a 2008 Catalyst study even proved this in relation to women at multinational corporations).[1] Broad institutional changes are necessary to bring about equality in the workplace, and no one person can make up for systemic problems, especially by just giving advice.

I hope that I've made you a firm disbeliever in the mentor myth. You're not a lost cause if you don't have a mentor. There's no need to spend hours on the Internet reading about how to chat up prospective mentors or attending networking events with your mentor radar turned up to eleven. That said, a mentor can be very helpful if you find a good match and understand how to work with your mentor to your benefit.

Working with Your Mentor

While a mentor may not be a necessity, there can certainly be value to cultivating a strong relationship with a more experienced person who can act as a sounding board and offer guidance. So how do you go about building a healthy, constructive, and effective mentor–mentee relationship? Let's start at the ground level. First, you have to find a mentor. I do not advocate making this an active search unless you are starting a business, making a significant upward leap, or switching industries and need specialized advice to guide you through the process. In general, trying to force a mentor relationship is a good way to ensure it will end up uncomfortable and ineffective. Either you are part of a formal mentoring program or you will meet someone whose advice you respect in the course of networking and doing business.

People tend to focus on finding mentors in their same

industry and function, but I don't think this is necessary. One of my favorite anecdotes about a successful mentor relationship comes from Allie Kline, CMO of AOL, Inc.[2] The man who ended up being her most important mentor was in the same industry but in a totally different department and job. She was interested in digital marketing, while he was in sales. As she tells it, she wanted to know more about digital technologies, while he didn't have a technical background. But his personal commitment to understanding her and her career goals in the long term made his coaching valuable. This type of mentoring is much more effective than mentoring that's confined to a veteran simply regurgitating stories about "what I did to get here." In this instance, the mentor truly understood and considered the needs of his mentee.

When looking for a mentor, do not confine yourself to more experienced people whose résumé is just a built-up version of yours. Look for mentors who can help you build the skill set you need (and if you are not sure what that skill set is, look for mentors who can help you understand what you need to know how to do). Sometimes the best wisdom you can learn from a mentor is processes, not skills. For example, how does your mentor make decisions? How does she manage her time or build relationships with staff, peers, and executives?

Apart from those facilitated through a formal mentoring program, the best mentor–mentee relationships are the ones that are built organically. Mentor–mentees should be matched by similar interests and a good rapport. Sometimes you will even meet mentors in less formal ways, like at the gym or in a recreational group. Having that common bond is important. A mentor is only going to take time out of her busy schedule to check in on you if she genuinely likes you and wants to see you succeed—if she feels connected to you and your success. Stilted coffee meetings where you pelt your mentor with rapid-fire questions don't make for a pleasant interaction. You should be able to visit with your mentor like you would a trusted friend. There just happens to be a profes- sional dimension to this relationship.

It should go without saying, then, that unless you're part of a formal program, you don't need to "define the relation- ship" with your mentor. Sheryl Sandberg has a great story about this. There was a young woman whose career she took an active interest in, helping her make big career decisions. After several years the young woman explains that she never had mentors to guide her in her professional choices. Sheryl wondered what she had been doing the last few years that didn't meet this young woman's expectations of mentorship.[3]

So how often do you need to meet with your mentor? There are no hard-and-fast rules. Approaching your mentor only when you are about to make a big career decision isn't smart—you want him to have a good sense of your working life outside times of transition. Maybe you grab coffee once a month (offer to pay) interspersed with phone calls, etc. You have to walk a fine line between keeping your mentor in the loop and being a burden on his time. If there is an activity that you both enjoy, like cycling or golfing, invite him to do that. Be prepared to take a long-term stance on growing this relationship. If you're the only one initiating contact, this may not be a mentorship worth pursuing.

Often, I see advice about talking to your mentor couched in interview-style questions. While reading these lists is a good way to get you thinking about the kinds of things you can use your mentor for, please do not actually talk to her this way. Being interviewed—unless the interviewer is excellent—is uncomfortable. If you want your mentor to talk about her most personal experiences in her career, you have to have a good interpersonal foundation. Allow time for the relationship to evolve, and be prepared to put in a lot of effort. The best mentor–mentee relationships take years to come to fruition.

The primary function of your mentor is to act as a sounding board, which is why it is important that you choose wisely. Just because your mentor gives you advice doesn't mean you have to follow it, but be considerate. And finding yourself repeatedly ignoring or regretting taking your mentor's advice is a sign that the mentorship is not the right fit. I see this most often when a person chooses a mentor based on his title or prestige. Be aware, especially if you are an entrepreneurial person, that someone with a C-level title at a large company might not share your appetite for risk. A tradition-bound executive's advice could be on the conservative side, and he might discourage you from taking risks that have the potential to pay off. Finding a mentor who shares or understands your values, even if this means he is younger or less titled than you might expect, is important.

When your mentor does give you great advice, make sure she understands how valuable her assistance is to you. Don't be shy about sending handwritten thank-you notes or small gifts as a way to express your thanks. Go above and beyond if she asks you to do something for her. The best mentoring relationships will continue to evolve into more equal relationships, in which both people are bringing their professional experiences and expertise to the table. You know when you have established a mentor–mentee relationship with depth when you mentor is calling you to ask for your perspective. In my experience, getting direct advice from a mentor should not be the objective of your relationship. The best mentors help you hone your thinking, examine opportunities or challenges strategically, ask tough questions, and provide tough love and feedback when others aren't willing to. Most importantly, good mentors share their experiences and offer a perspective on yours.

A final note: mentor–mentee relationships at times do end, although not usually in the "break up with your mentor" way that articles describe. This is most troublesome in formal mentoring programs. In the introduction I described my experience with a mentor who was actually harming my career, a situation that needed to be handled delicately. However you choose to move on from such a mentor, be graceful about it. There's no need for a dramatic confrontation (or any kind of confrontation). Usually, it is best to let the relationship just peter out. You may also find that you have people interested in becoming your mentor—usually a superior at your company—whom you do not want as a mentor. Maybe your values do not align, or perhaps you do not want this person influencing your decision making. This is a scenario you should handle carefully. Establish a professional friendship that does not confer the authority of a mentor. Or, if you are worried that any kind of relationship with the person will reflect poorly on you, figure out how to keep her at arm's length, whether that is limiting social time together or looking for projects the person is not involved in.

Sponsors

Even more valuable than a traditional mentor is a *sponsor*, someone who will actively promote you and your work. These are your champions, your biggest fans, who don't hesitate to tell others how great you are. While you can probably get by without a mentor, you will almost always need a sponsor if you're going to be successful. In the corporate world, your sponsor will put your name forth for promotions or great assignments. If you are an entrepreneur, your sponsor is the "raving fan" who recommends your business to prospective customers.

The impact of having a sponsor is material. Measuring people's level of satisfaction with their rate of advancement, 70 percent of men and 68 percent of women with sponsors are happy with their progress, up 19 percent and 23 percent respectively from the "unsponsored" men and women.[4] Additionally, 67 percent of men and 70 percent women without sponsors are unlikely to ask their managers for a raise, while 50 percent of sponsored men and 38 percent of sponsored women will do so.[5] Sponsorship shows an increasingly positive effect on statistics like asking for stretch assignments or general career trajectory.

Sponsors differ from traditional mentors in key ways (although your best mentors can become sponsors). Sylvia Ann Hewlett, a sponsorship expert, writes that mentors are people who know you well and help develop your leadership capabilities—they are people you jive with personally. Sponsors, on the other hand, may not be people whose leadership style you would like to emulate or who you have a close personal bond with. In other words, you don't have to like your sponsors, they just need to have the desire and ability to champion your work. Because of this, the most effective sponsors have a lot of power in an organization. Hewlett explains that in smaller companies your sponsor should ideally be the person at the top of the food chain, the company president or CEO. In larger companies, your sponsor should be positioned about two levels above you.[6]

So what should a sponsor be able to do on your behalf? A 2011 study titled "The Sponsor Effect" laid out sponsorship responsibilities as follows: advocating for their protégé, expanding the perception of what the protégé can do, making connections to senior leaders, promoting the protégé's visibility, opening up career opportunities, offering advice about executive presence, making connections outside the company, and giving advice.[7] Note that sponsorship is a two-way street. Your sponsor is promoting you with the expectation that you are bringing excellent work and a different perspective to her organization. If you decide to pursue sponsorship, make sure you are aware of the high-intensity commitment you are making to your company.

Finding a sponsor isn't always an easy undertaking. For example, I don't recommend asking someone to be your sponsor. This puts the person in an awkward spot if she doesn't have a natural belief in your talents. It is a bit like having a paid endorser versus a brand ambassador who promotes a product because he uses it and genuinely believes in it. The best advocates are always the latter. In other words, your sponsors should be self-appointed.

Many large companies have set up formal sponsorship programs because of the proven benefit of sponsors, especially for women and minorities. These programs are great and can certainly help keep your name at the forefront of conversations. But I believe the best sponsors find you. The best sponsors are those who recognize that you are worth putting their name on the line for. You earn the right to seek sponsorship by laying an excellent foundation with your work and by making your goals clear to people who are in a position to help you achieve them. So, a great second step (after competently executing on your assigned work) is to make your ambitions known by working your goals into conversations. If someone takes an interest in your desire to become a CPO or start a consultancy, get him involved. You should always have an answer to the question, "How can I help?"

One word of caution: in the event your potential sponsor decides to vet you with your manager, your manager must have excellent things to say about you and your performance. But sponsors can also offer a strategic way to work around incompetent managers. If you are looking to expand your role at your company and your manager is less than supportive, your sponsor can help you by mandating you are given certain assignments—but handle this carefully. Remember that your manager's reluctance may not be personal. He might just really need you in your current role or know you too well in that position to recognize your potential outside of your demonstrated skills. This is a particular challenge for women, who are often evaluated on past accomplishments, while men are generally evaluated on potential.

I've experienced this mode of evaluation for promotion firsthand. When I applied for a corporate role, which represented a departure from an operations role as a managing partner of a high-volume business, the president of the company interviewed me, had me do practice assignments to establish a track record, and got buy-in from his executive team (which I would become part of). Only after I was offered the position did I learn that my manager had vocally opposed my promotion on the grounds that I wasn't ready for such a big leap because I hadn't had exposure to the kinds of work I would be doing in my new role. Luckily, the president chose to make his decision based on what he believed my potential to be. With this vote of confidence, I worked my hardest to excel in the role and prove my old manager wrong.

Sponsorship is critical in organizations that value climbing the ladder, but it is still important if you are flying solo as an entrepreneur or small business owner. Research about obtaining sponsorship and the effectiveness of sponsorship outside of corporate structures is sparse. My view is that you want powerful people in your community and industry to champion you. It also helps to get third-party validation like "40 under 40" awards or other types of media exposure for the community work you do. This kind of recognition helps you get introduced to potential big customers or get access to exclusive networking groups. As you build your network, search out people who have the clout to make a difference in your trajectory. Convincing these people that it is worth their time to promote you will be key in your success.

One final thought on sponsorship: while you don't have to like your sponsor, your sponsor does have to like you. Often, you get a sponsor by being helpful and likable (not for bringing in cookies or doing office housekeeping). In order for someone to be a great sponsor, he has to be your diehard fan. This will only happen if he likes you and if you are helpful to him or his team and he wants to return the favor. Some of my biggest sponsors have been people I didn't help directly; instead, I helped *their children* with advice on their careers or on getting out of sticky professional situations. This should only underscore that people most want to promote you when you have been helpful to them with no explicit agenda.

Peer Mentors

As I help young professionals grow their careers, I find that peer mentorship is as valuable as traditional mentorship. Most literature about mentoring assumes that mentors are much older than mentees. I do not discount the value of experience, but some of the best ideas, experience sharing, and cautionary tales come from people close in age to yourself. Just to note, peer mentorship can take many different forms: mastermind groups, forums, or supper clubs. The purpose is the same, though—to bring like-minded individuals (usually seven to ten people) together around the common goal of supporting one another in their ambitions.

No one can better empathize with where you are in your career than people who are going through the same experiences you are. Hindsight gives the wearer rose-colored glasses—this is true of our view of our professional experiences as well. Older, more experienced mentors may look back fondly on their early years of drudgery, whereas your peers will know when your situation is appropriately challenging or a waste of effort. Traditional mentors may not be in a position to judge whether your hundred-hour weeks are unusual in your entry-level investment banking analyst position, as they are too far removed. However, your friend who works at a different investment bank will have her own experience to speak from.

Similarly, you can use your peer mentors as a barometer for the kinds of skills you should have and how advanced those skills should be. Are all the other digital marketers your age proficient in HTML5? Then you probably should be, too. Is every other female programmer part of a certain networking program in your city? Join it. This kind of group-think is positive, because it introduces you to new skills and opportunities that you might not have known about if you were not tapped into what your peers were doing.

Peer mentors also have the advantage of being more up to date on how technological innovation has affected your industry than a traditional mentor might be. This is not always true—I have known my fair share of technology mavericks in their advanced years—but I have also known plenty of older professionals who cannot seem to grasp the impact of an increasingly digital workplace. If you are in an industry that is subject to technological disruption (which is most industries), the input of your peers is critical. You want to be connected to the people who best understand the value of innovation, so you can plan for change and take advantage of the opportunities that arise in an evolving marketplace.

As you advance in your career, the types of peer mentors you have will progress from people who are allied with you in the struggle to break free from entry-level roles to people who can empathize with the difficulty of being a new manager, director, or even founder. When you find yourself at one of these points, I highly recommend finding a peer mentoring group made up of people with similar ambition levels but not necessarily the same career (so there's no direct competition). If you have just founded a technology business, join a peer mentor group of other entrepreneurs at various stages of their journey. A large circle of people with varying experiences and perspectives provides a crucial support network as you navigate new waters.

I am part of the Young Presidents' Organization, a global network of young chief executives. While the networking aspect is useful and fun, I find that being able to confidentially discuss the difficulties of scaling an organization is enormously helpful. Some of the challenges of being a young executive are surprising. Talking to people in similar situations helps me understand the right course of action and where the best resources are. I also run Lean In Circles with high-powered young women in major metropolitan areas. I find that these groups are much more effective than the standard networking coffee meetings between two people. Assembling a group of peers at similar levels creates a much more open dynamic. The emphasis is not on trying to impress the person sitting across from you; instead, as common experiences emerge, people seem to feel more comfortable sharing the difficulties they have at work. Getting feedback from not one but many people is also much more valuable, and leads to more solutions and ideas. I am consistently impressed by the dialogue that evolves in these groups.

I believe in the value of experience, but this does not mean you can't get great advice from people your own age or near you in age. Some of the best advisors you have will be only a level up from you. For them, the struggle is fresh, so their advice will be the most relevant. Watch the journeys of your peers to figure out what works and what doesn't. This is much easier than trying every management technique or speaking class yourself. And, most importantly, join a peer mentoring group. The combination of great networking and feedback makes participation in these kinds of circles invaluable.

Role Models

My final advice on network building relates to the most remote yet powerful aspects of your network: role models. Mentors, sponsors, and peer mentors all have an interpersonal element, but that is not required in order for a role model to be useful. You can have as many role models as you like, with no element of maintenance. They offer the most free, least intensive form of career advice you can find.

Most people know and understand what a role model is. You have probably idolized some hero from a young age. The professional value of role models is that they show you a proven path to achieving your ambitions. You want to move from hero worship to a critical understanding of what has made your role model successful. Many professionals I work with seem to feel the need to forge their own path. That's okay, but the smartest thing you can do is look at the journeys of your role models and pick and choose the pieces that work for you. Make an obsessive study of their careers. Read their autobiographies, listen to their earnings calls, and follow their social media accounts (if they have them). Develop a strategy based on what has worked—and learn from what hasn't. Their mistakes will be as valuable to you as their successes. What did your role models study in school? Did they go to business school? How did they break into the role or industry that eventually made their career? For example, if you want to be an astronaut, a notoriously difficult thing to become, look at how your astronaut heroes went about obtaining their jobs. What did they study and whom did they know? You want to develop a critical business understanding of how they built their success.

Your own professional journey will have unique elements, but you can copy strategically from the successes of others. Instead of just putting Warren Buffett on a pedestal, spend time analyzing what it is about his approach that impresses you. Pick and choose from his investment or organizational philosophies. Innovation is important, but reinventing the wheel is a waste of time. Your role models' journeys and worldviews are your first and best source of wisdom for your own career. Studying your role models is not just about the intangibles; you can draw advice from their presentation as well. Look at the way your role model dresses and behaves, without crossing the line into strange behavior. Recall the earlier example of former Secretary of State Madeleine Albright, whose pin collection added a personal flourish to her power suits. Steve Jobs's trademark jeans and black turtleneck make a statement about the importance of a sleek yet casual uniform.

If you are still trying to figure out what your career goals are, your role models should hint at what it is you would like to be doing. A role model's exact title may not fit you quite right, but perhaps an aspect of his career speaks to you. If you are trying to climb the ladder at a large company but your role models are Elon Musk and Steve Jobs, the corporate life may not be where your path lies. They are not your roles models because you want to make electric cars or smartphones but because you are drawn to founding your own company or working for an early-stage start-up. Similarly, if you are looking for the courage to take a big risk like quitting a stable job and starting a company, your role models' choices should be a source of encouragement. What did they risk and how did their risk taking pay off? Pick and choose what works for you. Personally, I look at the way people I admire execute their lives, especially how they integrate professional life and personal life. There are some role models I look to for their fitness regimes, while others I track for their executive presence, career path, or social media practices.

Finally, you do not have to have a close personal relationship with role models for them to be valuable. However, the glory of digital communication is that everyone is an e-mail away. With a little sleuthing, you should be able to find most people's contact information. If your role model is currently living, there is no harm in contacting him or her as long as you have an engaging story (your personal brand) to tell. Some of the most interesting mentor–mentee relationships, like that of Warren Buffett and Benjamin Graham, have developed this way. The worst that will happen is that you don't get a response.

Putting It All Together

You will spend your entire career building and improving your network of mentors, peer mentors, sponsors, and role models. One big mistake that people make in building a network—after continuing to network indiscriminately—is to consider their network a static rather than a dynamic resource. Networking is iterative. You will learn to be a better networker—to identify high-value targets and convince them to help you—as you continue to practice.

Another, and perhaps the largest, mistake people make is to network for what they can get from others. Most people know when they are being approached just so the networker can get something out of them. This is very off-putting. True networking is about building connections that are enjoyable and mutually beneficial. Always start with building relationships and asking how you can help the other person, not the other way around. Good mentors or sponsors will find ways to return the favor.

Mentors or sponsors will come in and out of your life as your career evolves. The best mentors will also become sponsors and friends, and will introduce you to their own highly vetted contacts. Other mentors may be truly worthwhile when you are in your twenties, but you may no longer keep in touch once you move to a certain level. Your strategy for deciding which resources you should put your time into will be a practiced study. Build your personal team of supporters the way you would any management team for a business: strategically, and with an eye for how they add value to your professional development.

CHAPTER 7

Overpromise, Overdeliver

As I was flipping through my Instagram account recently (just doing a casual brand audit!), I came across a photo of myself sitting at my desk wearing workout clothes and noise-cancelling headphones. The time stamp on the photo was 3:00 a.m. on a Saturday.

I don't usually spend my Friday nights/Saturday mornings chained to my desk; it's exhausting, generally unnecessary, and a bad example of work–life integration. But my company had committed to a deadline for a client that we had to deliver on.

The story goes like this: I was assisting a great client with processing their employee survey data. The project was assigned to an employee of mine, and I estimated it would take about a week to complete. She was given two weeks, because I knew she had other tasks to fulfill. During the two-week period I checked in a few times, and she said she was on track. Then, on Friday afternoon (the project was due on a Monday), she called me to say she was sorry but she had underestimated the time it would take her to complete the project—she wouldn't be finished by Monday. Her solution was to call the client and ask for another week. I knew she was going away for the weekend, so working overtime wasn't an option.

I never expect anyone to give up an important weekend for work, but I do expect all employees to deliver on their commitments and to call in support from coworkers if they cannot get a task done. Telling a client we are going to miss a deadline is not an option. I told her not to worry about it—I would handle it. I asked two other staff members I knew would be interested in overtime if they could help out. Together, we worked all weekend (including the documented all-nighter for me). We finished the project by Sunday morning, and the client never knew what we had to go through to deliver on the deadline. The cool thing was that we actually had a lot of fun rallying as a team and getting the work done, especially with the "boss" (me) getting down in the weeds.

In our hyperconnected world, every professional action you take has significance. This is why it is imperative that you do your job well, that you make professional commitments carefully, and that you overdeliver on every commitment you make. When you take a job, you are committing to do that job. When you ask for extra work, you shouldn't do it as lip service to your ambition. When you tell someone you are going to call him, do it. Quality, timeliness, and reliability are the adjectives you want associated with you and your work products. You don't get those labels unless you overpromise and overdeliver every single time.

If you take nothing else away from this book, it should be the idea that you are personally accountable for your career. We have talked about commitment, the myth of the magic mentor, and learning to manage your time—these are all tools and strategies you need to take control of your career. But you also need to make two promises to yourself in your daily work in order to succeed. The first is to never do the bare minimum. The second is to always deliver on your commitments.

Rejecting the Bare Minimum

I have learned in my career that you have to be careful about giving universal career advice about how people should do their day jobs. Everyone's situation is different. But this wisdom I stand by, no matter what: never, ever do the bare minimum. Going beyond the minimum relates specifically to the work expected of you. We have discussed how to optimize your time and work for impact by strategically choosing roles that are in line with your larger goals. This advice is specifically about how to do the best you can at the job you have with an attitude that will help you win in all facets of your life.

Conquering 'Boring Tasks'

Rejecting the bare minimum should be an attitude that starts from day one of your career, although often it isn't. When people begin a new job, they seem to believe that the work required of them is fully covered by the job description they responded to in the job posting. Understand that a written job description covers the basics of what you will doing, but it is neither comprehensive nor static. Sometimes the extra responsibilities added to your actual work will be engaging and skill building; sometimes they will be boring and below your ability level. Either way, you have committed to getting them done.

The unexpected drudgework is what I hear complaints about most often in my consulting work. People can't believe the note taking, database management, etc. that they are asked to do. Remember when I said you should be strategic about the projects you take on at work and try to avoid busy work? I meant it. But that doesn't give you a blank check to reject the less glamorous work you don't like. I understand that it can be frustrating to spend time on low-level tasks that are outside your strict job description when you are trying to kick butt at your position. When you took this job, though, you made an implicit commitment to deliver on the work asked of you. Even if you don't love that work, don't throw a fit and complain. If you play your cards right, these tasks will not be yours forever.

There's a strategy here, and it goes like this: when you start a job, especially an entry-level job, you won't have much explicit control over what you work on. So, this means you will sometimes get stuck working on stuff that is neither fun nor career boosting, aka Boring Tasks. Don't neglect Boring Tasks, and make sure no one knows how much you hate them. You're doing them exactly because they are boring and no one else wants to do them. It should look very, very easy for you to accomplish these mundane tasks. I even recommend getting a portion of your Boring Tasks done out of sight so people don't think of you as just the person who works on, for example, reconciling contact data. Arrive early, stay late— just make sure the Boring Task is never something your manager has to remind you to do. Deliver on it consistently *and* excellently. Hopefully, your manager will be both grateful you've taken it off her hands and impressed with your ability to buckle down and get stuff done.

But don't worry—you're not going to have to do the Boring Task forever! Part of the reason you want to do Boring Tasks outside your normal working hours is to free up workday time for new projects. Make the case to your boss about which projects you can add business value to. Strategically advocate for work that is high-impact and interesting. Kill at getting those extra projects done, too, being the committed worker that you are. If you excel at the more advanced projects you take on, you will eventually become too valuable for Boring Tasks. Just by being great at your job and showing you are committed to helping in any way you can, you have expanded your responsibilities. A delicate conversation that highlights how your chosen projects add business value can help shift your responsibilities away from the Boring Tasks you don't like. Just make sure to choose your moment. Too soon, and your manager will think you're feeling entitled about work. Too late, and you will be stuck as a worker bee.

Notice above that I said that you must get your work done consistently *and* excellently. Finishing your work and doing an excellent job is the bare minimum, not just finishing. You must do your work *well*. Your work product should always be functional, accurate, and presentable. If you find yourself only checking the box on certain projects, you need to reexamine your approach to them. There is a chance that the task has become rote to you because it is fairly simple. If so, strategize ways you can automate the task. For example, if one of your jobs is to build a report, think about whether you can build a macro that does the report for you with just the press of a key instead of requiring that you input data manually.

Another helpful trick to try if you aren't feeling motivated by a task is to remind yourself how the task connects to your larger mission. What bottom line does it contribute to? Does it help the company analyze ROI? Is it a small but fundamental part of a very important process? If I am having trouble finding the focus do something really well, going through the thought process of why it is important gets my head back in the game. Sometimes the answer is that the task actually *isn't* that important anymore; it's not uncommon for company processes to become ingrained and stale. We hand down Excel reports or paperwork flows like we hand down holiday traditions. Sometimes they need to change, but someone must first notice and explain why they are no longer relevant before change comes. If you believe you have been tasked with a dinosaur of a work flow, explain to your manager why the process is broken and what you could be doing instead. As long as you bring a seamless efficiency to your function (and as long as it doesn't sound like you're complaining), your manager will probably be amenable.

Doing your assigned work and then some is how people understand that you are ready for new challenges and opportunities. Don't ever think of your job as only the five bullet points written down on an interview posting. Reject the bare minimum by taking care of what people expect of you and then going beyond.

Above and Beyond: The Extra 10 Percent

Because you are the captain of your fate, you should have a strategy in place for what work ends up being your responsibility. Rejecting the bare minimum doesn't mean you go crazy doing any and all work that presents itself. Don't forget the advice we discussed in chapter 4, "Everything Speaks: Personal Brand Matters." Work hard, but don't fall victim to the popular fallacy that long hours in the office every day are the best way to show off your value. Too often, people believe that complaining about their long hours and how hard they work will convince their coworkers and managers how valuable they are. This is not true. If you operate as if all available bandwidth is being taken by your mundane work, your manager won't be comfortable assigning you more challenging work.

You show your business value by going above and beyond on every assignment given to you. No one is going to make you do your job. If you are being micromanaged, it is probably because you aren't performing well (there is also a chance your manager is inexperienced, in which case you should have a nuanced conversation with your manager about your responsibilities and the kind of oversight you feel comfortable with). If you are not getting your work done well, it can easily be assigned to someone else and then you have "lost" a great business opportunity to prove your worth. So get your work done, ask for help when you need it, and keep an eye out for opportunities to add extra value.

Actually, this is an attitude you should cultivate in your everyday life. The more you practice overdelivering, the more your attitude will carry over into your professional life. Run an extra lap. Hit an extra bucket of golf balls. Spend an extra fifteen minutes at the piano. Plan on an extra act of kindness for your partner, kids, or friends. This will train your brain to look at a situation and figure out the best way for you to expand upon what is being asked of you. These small things will be noticed and will build your reputation as someone who goes above and beyond.

We Are Talking Once Again About Commitment

Remember the final C in our Four Cs, commitment? This time there is a subtle difference in the way we are using the word. This isn't a high-level, esoteric philosophy of commitment that motivates you to stay true to your company and your mission. Commitment here really just means doing what you say you will do. It's that simple. Which is why it's so confusing that so few people follow through on their commitments. How many times do you hear, "I will call you," "I will make the introduction to so and so," or "I will send you a copy"? And how many times do you receive the call, introduction, or copy? How many times have you sat in a strategy meeting during which everyone agrees on wonderful and actionable objectives—and nothing happens?

From personal experience, I know how infrequently people follow through on their stated intent. I can't tell you why this happens. Perhaps they don't consider these statements to be real commitments, or perhaps we are all just too busy and distracted, so we forget. I think neither of these excuses works. If you say you are going to do something, do it. And if you are prone to forgetfulness, create a system that helps you track and execute on your commitments.

I know the difference between the people I can count on to follow up 100 percent of the time and everyone else. That kind of commitment is meaningful to me as a businessperson. If you always execute on the commitments you make, that tells me that you have both integrity and an attention to detail that touches all of your business dealings. I don't think it is an accident that my hundred-percenters are also some of the busiest and most successful people I know. These people take responsibility not only for their own commitments but for their employees' as well. One CEO I know ordered carbon copy notepads and carried them with him to every meeting. If anyone committed to an actionable idea, he wrote it down on the notepad, gave the employee the top copy, and posted the carbon on the "Accountability Board" displayed in the office. The copy stayed up until the employee had executed on the commitment. This might sound extreme, but it was very effective.

My challenge for you is to make your own personal pledge right now that you will only commit to things you intend to follow up on, and to always follow up on things you commit to. Your stated intentions mean something to the people around you, and you should not underestimate how much. The casual "I will e-mail you" might be something you said without thinking much of it. You intend to e-mail that person on your timeline, which could be never. The thing about these casual commitments is that even if the matter isn't terribly important to the person you promised an e-mail or introduction to, she *will* remember if you don't do it—and that will matter. People who depend on you, like your manager or investors, will notice most of all, and they will begin to make value judgments about your reliability. Once set, these judgments are very hard to change. Mess up once or twice by forgetting to follow through, and that's enough to negate an otherwise solid track record. But if you are consistent, you will reap the rewards. You will be tasked with the important things a company can't afford to have go sideways, because people know you can be counted on to deliver.

If you make a commitment, do everything in your power to make it happen. There have been many times that I have come close to not delivering something I promised. Most people probably would have explained the extenuating circumstances and asked for more time. Instead, I pulled all-nighters, moved vacations, and brought in temp staff. This is how serious I am about following up on my commitments. These extreme measures were not common for me; usually, I am able to execute on my promises without going to these crazy lengths because I manage my time thoughtfully and understand my constraints. So, don't get disheartened if you are starting to think that a successful career means sacrificing everything while moving at breakneck speed all the time. All-nighters and the like should be the exception, not the rule. If you do end up staying up all night or moving a vacation, though, you send a strong message to your manager, client, or investors that you are all in.

Should you find yourself *continually* staying up all night or cancelling your vacation, there is a problem. I will kindly direct you back to chapter 3: "A Week Is 168 Hours—Use Them Wisely" for some time management strategies that will make your life more livable.

Finishing Projects Right

In your attempt to deliver what you promised, you will also be judged on *how you bring a project to a close.* Do you wrap things up on time? Are there loose ends? Is there appropriate supporting documentation in place so that someone else could easily take over the work product or assess its business value? Have you built a system that notifies anyone who engages with your work product of errors or reports on returns? If it was an especially large project, did you hold a final meeting to discuss with your team how well the work product met your goals? Did you meet the objectives you decided upon in your kickoff meeting? I can't tell you how often I come across people who start projects but never quite finish them. Redesigning websites, updating a company's filing systems (digital or otherwise), creating a new year-end reporting system, implementing KPIs (key performance indicators) or dashboards, updating a company's user manual— these are just a few projects that I see drag on and on.

When the work is naturally iterative, it is especially hard to decide when and how to be finished. I see this most often in creative work and software design. The artist/writer/designer/developer can go on and on perfecting an already good project. This is why it is important to have project objectives laid out before you begin. When you have hit those objectives, you are done. Adding scope to a project is a dangerous thing and can compromise your ability to effectively deliver on your promises. If the bells and whistles are part of your "extra 10 percent" then go ahead and add them, but don't flub a deadline in order to get them in.

The interesting thing is that it is difficult to get fired for being one of those people who never quite wraps up the big things he is working on. Unless the project has a very obvious deadline, like the company's annual shareholders' meeting, it can be unclear when a project is really finished. People who don't finish their work always seem busy because they are always working on something, though it's the same thing they've *been* working on. Usually, they have made the product or system so complex that it is difficult to bring anyone else in to oversee it. They can fly under the radar for years, becoming a huge resource drain for the company. Management turnover in many companies is so high that most managers don't last through a long-term project's whole life cycle, so there is no consistent oversight (management turnover might even contribute to these projects getting so drawn out).

The worst situation is to get stuck under a manager who operates this way, forever shifting focus, adding scope, and never finishing the projects he has started. This is a great way to stall your career. When you're not able to truly finish products, you can't show executives concrete deliverables that support your bid for promotion. If you find yourself in this situation, I believe it is best to switch teams if you can. You don't want to be associated with people who spin their wheels and don't add real value to the company. Even if you have a stable job, believe me when I say you are not going anywhere.

Managing Up and Out

Delivering on your commitments can be very complex if you are not the only person responsible for the final work product. Everyone has been on that project team in school with one or more team members who just wouldn't pull their weight for the final group project. Does that suck? Yes. But a bad team member is not an excuse for failing to execute on your commitments. Working around weak links in a team is part of learning how to work effectively in a team environment. The further up the corporate ladder you go or the more experience you have as a business owner, the more variations you will see in the skills, motivations, and styles of other people.

If you are lucky, you will have been graced with team members who are equally ambitious and committed. Making sure they deliver is more a matter of coordination than motivation. Kicking off a project with a meeting that creates clarity for goals, timeline, and work flow is a great idea—it gets everyone on the same page from the outset. Using a project tracking software during the project (if the project is involved) is smart, too. I know many teams, technical and otherwise, that do a daily scrum to catch everyone up on individual progress. Knowing where each team member is in terms of project milestones is a must, so you don't hit a deadline and realize that one of your team members has dropped the ball. Make sure you walk that fine line between holding people accountable and being a nag. You probably don't enjoy being overmanaged either, so trust your team members to deliver on their commitments, while still having a firm idea of what they are up to. If the work they deliver is not up to the quality you prefer, and if you aren't right up against a deadline, take time to explain how and what you would like done differently. Most often people aren't being lazy—they just were not clear on your vision.

The trouble comes when you are faced with one or more team members or—even worse—a manager who either does not share your commitment to delivering an excellent and timely work product or is not as motivated as you are. This is a very difficult situation to manage, especially if you are managing up. Your commitment must still be to getting the work done, even if you have to shoulder extra weight. In these situations, those all-nighters or weekends at the office come into play. But you don't want such extraordinary efforts to become the norm—your team members should not expect that you will always come through for them. One way to deal with this problem is to carefully document the project deliverables and who worked on each aspect for what amount of time. You can either make this public so your manager can draw her own conclusions about people's participation, or you can request a meeting with your manager and explain, without complaining, how the workload was actually distributed.

When you have a manager who is flaky about deadlines or does not have the same eye for detail that you do, your position can be even more difficult. Even if you get her to commit to a project timeline, there is no guarantee she will stick to her promises, since she has the final deciding power. I have dealt with this a few times and found it was smart to find high-visibility projects with other power players and do a great job on those, so people in the company learned to trust my personal abilities and ethic (while I still got my own work done). That way, when my team's long-term projects didn't get finished because of my manager's stonewalling, the people in charge of promoting me knew it was not my fault.

You can also go to a senior person in your organization with whom you have a great relationship and ask for help in working with your manager. Explain the situation and that delivering on projects is really important to you. Make sure the person you confide in understands that you are not complaining, you just need advice to solve the problem. This way, if your team's lack of follow-through ever comes up in a senior leadership meeting you will have someone who knows your side of the story.

One Step Further: Challenging Yourself

Once you have mastered going beyond the bare minimum and following up on all your commitments, you can take the next step in your quest to overdeliver. Start raising the bar on your commitments. After reading the early chapters of this book, you should already be in this mindset. This final step formalizes your personal "challenges."

How does this commitment to upping your goals work in real life? Don't just do what your manager asks—do it better. For example, if your manager comes to you and asks you to do an analysis on cutting 10 percent of your department's overheard costs, deliver a report that finds 12 percent of inefficiencies. If you are asked to make a presentation and deliver it within a week, have it ready in a couple days. Instead of hitting your sales quota, exceed it. And so on. If you are self-employed, stretching your goals works much the same way. Beating projected timelines, budgets, and deliverables are all ways to make your clients very happy.

Your attitude should be that you are going to get and give the most out of every encounter. You are all in. With your limited and excellently managed 168 hours, you don't have a choice but to make the most of every encounter, whether it is starting a new job, learning a new skill, or talking to a stranger on a plane. If you choose to challenge yourself to this degree, understand the trade-offs you are making in your life.

This is an intense commitment to your career. You can't tell your manager you want extra work and then routinely take long weekends. Chances are you can't deliver projects early without coming to work early or staying late. It is perfectly fine if you don't want to play at this level, just make sure the image you project of your commitment matches your actions. People will form initial opinions of you based on the former and judge you based on the latter.

Putting It All Together

The job market is growing increasingly competitive. The number of people with advanced degrees in the workforce is steadily growing. Lower-skilled jobs are being converted to automatic technical processes, and artificial intelligence will replace many additional jobs in the near future. A global, connected workforce allows skilled people to work remotely across borders—and to work all the time. All these factors together can make it feel like getting ahead is an upward battle.

I actually feel the opposite. Is there more competition? Sure. Do people work a lot more than they used to, enabled by cell phones and laptops? Yes. Sometimes, though, I feel that technology has made us as distracted as it has made us efficient. Many people get too caught up surfing social media or digital content (the "bored at work" network[1]), multitasking on projects, or looking for their next job to really deliver on what they've been assigned. Just by making your commitments explicit and following up with more than what was expected, you are ahead of the curve. The nice thing about excellence is that it becomes a habit if you practice consistently. Holding yourself to this standard of performance is what I mean by being all in. There is no halfway on this one; either you commit or you don't.

CHAPTER 8

Taking Action and Risks

We are at a special time in the evolution of work. Techno-logical advances and shifting generational expectations have created a more dynamic workforce. People will be working longer and changing jobs more than in previous generations.[1] Gone are the days of the "company man," a professional committed to spending the entirety of his professional exis-tence advancing in the ranks of one corporation. People who switched jobs, changed industries, or started companies were once viewed as rebels. This is no longer the case. That shift in attitude is even reflected in our modern-day professional heroes: we have moved from idolizing the Jack Welches of the world to lionizing the Mark Zuckerbergs.

Because a less linear career is now a given rather than a choice, you need to be comfortable embracing the risk inher-ent in professional transitions. I don't think this added level of uncertainty is bad. In fact, the opposite can prove true: big jumps are how you get ahead, whether you measure "ahead" by title, salary, total earning power, or your impact on the world. That idea is not based on anecdotal evidence alone. Research shows that employees, on average, receive a 3 percent salary bump annually.[2] A Wharton study found that external hires are paid, on average, about 20 percent more coming into a job than people at the same level who were brought up internally.[3]

The takeaway is that the best way to get ahead is no longer to find a ladder and climb it until you reach the top (or the highest rung you can reach). A professional journey is now more comparable to a series of ladders placed side by side. The fastest way to ascend is to occasionally hop off your ladder and onto the next one, reaching for an adjacent rung a little above what you could reach if you stayed on the ladder you were climbing. The hops between ladders are where you will see your greatest promotion in terms of title or salary. You will reach your goals far faster than if you had stayed on one ladder and kept plugging along.

Despite the lessons learned from this data and the prevailing positive attitude toward entrepreneurship, I still find that people tend to be overly conservative in their careers. They stay in jobs too long and fail to capitalize on opportunities for promotion. Even if people are brave enough to ask for a raise, they often don't make the argument well and their risk taking is not rewarded. I also believe that you can't make conservative people less risk averse, but you can give them frameworks to help them take more leaps.

Herein lies the key to this chapter: I am not telling you to love risk, but I will show you how to make riskier choices that pay off strategically. I will discuss times of universal transition: taking risks at work (asking for high-profile assignments or raises), switching jobs, switching industries, and starting businesses. Each requires a unique approach, a checklist of ways that you can make yourself more prepared for the leap, whether it is building a solid business case for a promotion or having all your ducks in a row when you finally launch your own small business.

A Note for the Cautious

We will spend this chapter dealing with risk as it applies to specific professional situations. Before we begin, I'd like to share some advice designed especially for the risk averse among us. I said in the introduction to this chapter that if you are a fundamentally conservative person, I can't change that. But there are two helpful pieces of advice I do have for you.

First, whenever you are faced with a "risky" choice like a decision to change jobs or to pursue a high-profile project at work, you need to ask yourself what the risk of *not* trying is. For example, if you've been working the same job for several years and a promotion does not seem imminent, what is the risk of *not* going out and looking for a new job? What if you end up working this job for ten more years? What if you are maxing out your earning potential? What if you get phased out because you aren't worth promoting and younger, hungrier workers are vying for your job? Repeat this exercise whenever you spot a career-advancing opportunity you are unsure about pursuing. You can apply this test to something as simple as the decision to send a networking e-mail to someone you admire. You might send that e-mail and not get a response, but if you don't send the e-mail in the first place you're ensuring that you won't get a response.

Second, as with building confidence, the more you challenge yourself and take risks, the more comfortable with risk taking you will become. You won't like it any more than you do now, but the scariness factor will diminish over time—or at least you'll get better at taking the plunge. Confidence and risk taking are inextricably tied. Taking low-level risks (i.e., sending e-mails) builds your confidence to the point that you can take big plunges like switching jobs.

Instead of beating yourself up about not being the kind of person who jumps without hesitation into uncharted waters, accept your tendencies—but not their limitations. When you find yourself balking at taking a leap, meditate on this question: What do I risk by **not** doing this? The answer is often that the risk of not taking action outweighs the risk of going ahead, even if everything goes wrong.

A Note for the Bold

Millennials get a bad rap for being flaky, entitled, and willing to change jobs at the drop of a hat. This reputation is true in specific cases, but it is more of a reflection of the new dynamic workforce than the general character of millennials.

While I am more concerned with people who take too few risks, it's possible to err in the opposite direction as well. If you are a young, ambitious person in an entry-level job, it is easy to get bored and restless. Switching jobs every time you get bored isn't strategically incorporating risk. So before you quit your latest job, do a full analysis of why you are dissatisfied and where there is room for growth in your current role. If you decide that there isn't any, then you can start looking for something new. In the coming years, we will see people switching jobs more and more frequently, but there is still such a thing as changing positions too frequently. No hard-and-fast rule exists, but a new job every six months sounds like a lot to me. There is a difference between taking on risk and being unfocused.

In addition, part of embracing risk is learning how to hedge it. Taking a huge risk like starting a company without having a backup plan isn't brave, it is foolish. The following sections are as useful for the overly brave as they are for the inherently timid. Your inclination might be to go for every exciting new opportunity you see. I will help you build risk into your career using a framework that proves the business value of the move you are making.

Embracing Risk at Work

It is a little odd to talk about embracing risk at your job. Part of the reason you have a job is that it offers a stable income (I am guessing). But if you only work within the confines of your position, you're never going to take that big jump that pushes you out of your current level and pay grade.

The trick is to rock the boat without capsizing it. Too many people show up at work day after day, then sit back and hope they will get noticed for the work they do. It doesn't seem fair, but hard work usually isn't enough to get you noticed. If you want better projects or a promotion, you need to put yourself out there and ask for them—but at the right time and in the right way.

Choosing High-Profile Projects and Roles

You might expect that doing an excellent job at assigned work would be enough to get you promoted, but it often isn't. You definitely need to take care of your assigned tasks, but in order to get noticed and catch the attention of high-level sponsors or mentors, you also need to find yourself high-profile projects that are going to put you in front of the people who have the power to advance your career.

Step one is always taking care of your assigned tasks. You can't ask for extra work or take on high-level projects if you're not killing it at your regular job. (I know I am repeating myself here, but I come across many people who forget they have to actually do their job. Before you start stepping up for challenging work, remember to do the stuff you were hired to do.)

So what do you do once you have mastered your assigned tasks? Where do you find the golden opportunities that will push you out of your comfort zone and into the limelight? Sometimes you can create these opportunities for yourself by pitching a project that seems warranted in the context of the company (there's nothing like showing a little initiative). Make sure, though, that your proposed project has your manager's blessing and doesn't take away from the hours you spend on the work you have. And make sure it's high impact. For example, only offer to do a task like reorganizing the company's files if it is going to win you brownie points with someone in the C-suite.

More often, you can take advantage of existing opportunities. This can be volunteering to lead a new initiative, organize a company retreat, or present for your department at the annual shareholder meeting. If you are not yet at the level to be awarded these things, offer to assist the person who is charged with giving the speech or leading the initiative. You want to keep your eyes and ears open for these opportunities because they usually won't just be handed to you. This is why it's useful to have connections at work outside your team. The better networked you are within the company, the more of these golden opportunities you will know about.

When it comes to putting yourself out there for these projects, it's usually simply a matter of convincing yourself to try—and try a few levels above what your natural inclination is. I tell my clients: don't apply for the subcommittee, apply to be chairman of the board. Even if you aren't made chairman, the secondary position you are offered will be much better than what you are naturally inclined to try for. Or—you never know—you might get the chairman position. Even if you feel like the position you are shooting for is beyond your abilities, trust the judgment of the people awarding the role. There's no quicker learning curve than picking up skills on the job.

Remember to pick projects for impact. You only have so much bandwidth and time. Type A professionals usually want to run everything, but the shotgun approach at work isn't smart. Choose work that is either pivotal to a core area of the business or will come under review by an executive. Giving presentations, either internally or at external events like customer appreciation conferences, is a great way to do this. Anytime you are standing up in front of people and saying smart things, you are promoting yourself. So many people fear public speaking that a willingness to take on these kinds of assignments is well rewarded. If you are unsure of your public speaking skills—or any skills that are important for taking on high-profile tasks—take a class or attend a training session. Staying within the confines of your current abilities is how you get stuck at an entry-level position.

Making a Business Case for a Raise

Putting yourself out there for high-profile projects feels like small potatoes compared with asking for a raise. This is a conversation that most people dread, and for good reason: most people go about it the wrong way and the exchange ends up being very uncomfortable. But it doesn't need to be. The biggest mistake people make is focusing the conversation on emotions or effort instead of results. This is not the time to discuss what is fair or what you deserve. It is a business conversation and should be focused as such. The right way to ask for a raise is to build a business case for why your employer should pay you more.

There are optimal times to ask for a raise as well. Usually, people get an annual bump to their base salary (or, as we call it in HR, COLA [cost of living allowance]). Contrary to common thought, this is not the time to negotiate with your manager for a raise. The chances of getting anything significantly above the standard package are low. The best times to negotiate a big raise are (1) when you are first offered the job or (2) when you are given a promotion. For example, research done in 2014 showed that employees on average would receive 3 percent raises (adjusted for inflation that came out to about 1 percent). However, employees who left an old job to begin a new one earned 10–20 percent more than their original pay.[4]

When you are building your business case for a raise, frame your argument by analyzing the value you add to the organization or the outside world. The first thing you want to know is your market value. What do people in your position earn on average in your industry? You can generally find this information on the Internet (be sure to consult a credible source) or tap a friend who works in HR. If you are being offered or paid far less than the average, it is acceptable to use this information as a bargaining chip—or a sign to seek employment elsewhere. Ask your manager how she arrived at the number she did or where the company makes up for a below-market salary in terms of total compensation. Make sure to bring the data you researched with you, in case you need backup. Remember, this negotiation is not about fairness; it is about proving why you should earn a certain compensation based on the business value you bring to the company and your value in the wider market.

While you should compare your earnings to the market as a whole, never compare what you earn to what your coworkers earn. Unless your company has a transparent compensation policy, this information is generally intended to be confidential. Managers hate it when employees justify a raise by saying, "Well, Suzie earns $90,000 and we have the same title, so I should be making at least that." You might have the same title, but Suzie may add more business value than you do, hence her bigger salary. Or she might have negotiated for the salary when she was hired. You never know the full story, and, frankly, it's not relevant to your situation. Plus, your manager will likely wonder what other confidential matters you discuss with your peers. You don't want to become the person your manager doesn't trust.

Similarly, never bring up how hard you work—and especially don't bring up how many hours you work. Either the hours are expected or your manager will wonder why it takes you so long to do your job. Working hard is a given. Instead, talk about specific projects you did that required effort outside the expectations of your role. Explain the value you have added via these projects. Managers like to have concrete, even data-driven, examples of why you deserve a certain level of compensation. Sometimes they have full control over what you make, but usually they have to take your argument to HR or their own manager for approval. It helps if you have built the case for your raise for them.

Finally, never, ever argue for a raise for personal reasons. Unfortunately, I often see this mistake, made mostly by women who ask for a raise a month or two after taking a job because they cannot afford rent or another personal expense. Again, it is up to you to know your market value and plan your lifestyle—including the salary you need to make and your budget for expenses. Instead of telling your manager you need to make a certain salary for personal reasons, just figure out your baseline and do not accept anything lower. Your internal math might be based on your personal expenses, but when you approach your manager you should structure your argument on the market and the value you can add.

Making the Case for a Promotion

The advice about asking for a raise also applies to asking for a promotion. Usually, promotions are offered to employees whose managers feel they are ready for the next career step, but if you feel like you can make the case, it is okay to ask your manager for a "title change" (this is a good way to phrase it).

Remember to respect the existing structure of titles that your company uses. Don't ask for anything off the wall or totally unreasonable. Some companies have set career milestones, such as a certain number of years working at the company or in a role, before an employee is promoted to the next level. Make sure to understand these rules before you approach your manager for a new title. Another smart thing to do is groom and train your replacement *before* you ask for the promotion. Too often, people are held back because they are so valuable in their existing role that the cost of replacing them would be onerously high.

If your company does not have such a formal structure, you will have an easier time asking for a title change. One good way to approach the discussion is by explaining that your title no longer matches your responsibilities. Perhaps your work has expanded in scope and you are no longer just a social media manager but a digital marketing manager. Make sure, when you frame your request, that your manager doesn't feel like you are trying to worm out of your less glamorous responsibilities.

A smarter, sneakier way to approach promotions is to schedule a meeting with your manager and, instead of asking for a promotion, ask what the requirements are for, as an example, a director's position at your company. If you have a checklist of the expectations for the position you want, you can use that list to build your skill set. Even better, when you do go to argue for that promotion, your manager has already given you the framework you need to make your case for why you add the kind of value a director does.

Looking for a New Job

Sometimes you will have exhausted all the opportunities at your current job. The key is knowing when to call it quits and make the jump to something new. As I've said, the most common mistake I see is people staying in jobs too long. So how do you know when to look for a new job?

If you are no longer challenged by your role, then it is time to start looking upward or outward. If you are ready to be promoted based on your technical skills but there isn't a role open in your company, don't wait for the role to open up or the company to grow—make the jump. If you are not aligned with company leadership's view of your performance, you either need a reality check or to go somewhere that believes in developing you.

This final scenario is one I want to address in more detail because I come across it so often. For whatever reason, even deserving people are sometimes not considered exceptional by their manager. Once you are assigned a performance bucket, it is very hard to escape it. This is great news if you are considered a top performer but bad news if you are thought to be mediocre or even lacking. This happens in school too: certain kids are labeled "smart" early on, even if they aren't. Other kids are thought to be not as bright. The underachievers might have trouble focusing or just didn't gel with their kindergarten teacher. Regardless, the label sets the tone for them going forward. What people think about us we tend to believe about ourselves. This can happen slowly, insidiously. One middling performance review might not do it, but a string of them could be enough to convince you that you aren't ambitious or effective. If you have a lukewarm review, either explore it in more detail with your manager or an objective third party, or start looking for a new job.

Starting a job hunt can be intimidating, but that is because most people take a depersonalized approach to finding a job. They rely solely on online postings that receive thousands of applicants and therefore they get more than their fair share of automated rejection e-mails. A better way to go about a job search is, as soon as you decide you are looking, to let people know you are open to opportunities—although you should wait to tell your manager until you are sure you are leaving, so be careful about this getting back to him. Tell your mentors, peers, friends, and even people you meet at networking events and conferences. You can never anticipate which connection will have a lead that turns into something real.

When you approach your contacts, make sure you have your angle figured out (once again, we are back to personal branding). What kinds of positions are you interested in? Why are you switching jobs? What sorts of growth opportunities do you want to pursue? Most of your answers will be informed by what you are lacking in your current job (keep this to yourself), but you can do a little outside research, too. Read the newspaper to identify what companies or industries are growing so you can target high-demand positions. Being able to articulate why, from an economic perspective, you are interested in getting in front of people at a certain company will help your business contacts connect you.

Even though we are discussing active job searches here, I think it is smart to always have your pulse on the job market. You are not being disloyal to your employer, you're just gathering data to better understand your market value. Make a point to read job postings every once in a while. You never know when your dream job is going to pop up—and it's much better to apply for a job when you don't need it than when you do (your bargaining power will be better). Checking job postings also lets you gather salary data; what are people hired for positions similar to yours being offered? Your research has the extra benefit of giving you ideas of additional duties that can expand or add value to your current role.

Whether or not you are looking for a job, make sure your résumé is updated (see "Seven Tips for a Great Résumé" on page 18 for help in keeping it polished). Keeping your résumé up to date is common business advice, but few people follow it. Take a look at your résumé right now—does it reflect your current responsibilities? In your bulleted explanations of your job, keep everything action based and business oriented. Don't be esoteric; name specific deliverables you were in charge of and their impact on the business. Be as quantitative as possible so those reviewing your résumé have context for the databases, budgets, and numbers of people you managed. If you have anything personal on there—hobbies or interests—delete them. They are taking up room that you could be using to highlight your business or philanthropic experience. The exception to this rule is if you are a gifted athlete with notable achievements that highlight your competitive and high-achieving personality.

If your excellent résumé and a warm introduction score you an interview, you now need to prepare yourself for meeting the hiring manager face to face. While some of your preparations will be about your personal presentation (see chapter 4, "Everything Speaks: Personal Brand Matters"), most of what you need to do is information gathering. Read everything you can get your hands on about your target company, the industry it is in, and how the macroeconomic climate affects both. Pay attention to the organization's annual reports, white papers, presentations, and social media feeds. In addition to gaining knowledge about the company, you are trying to figure out how your role fits into the company's evolving strategy. How will you help add value given where the company is going? Try to keep the conversation forward looking, explaining why your skills are useful for that organization.

When discussing your past experience, only say positive things. Even if you hated your previous job, this isn't the time to discuss it. If you need to explain why you are leaving your current job, use reasons like you are looking for a new challenge or you truly believe in this company's mission, rather than that you hate your manager. Keep the focus on projects you accomplished at your job rather than transactional activities. One more bit of research prep you can do: without crossing into creepy territory by checking personal sites, go ahead and look up your interviewer on LinkedIn or the company website to get a better sense of her (you can certainly ask the recruiter or HR person arranging your interview who you will be talking to). Such investigation used to be a socially uncomfortable practice, but it has become almost expected as digital networking has become more common. Rest assured, your interviewer will be Googling you.

Switching Industries

Sometimes a job switch is actually an industry switch. This is becoming increasingly common, as people become more specialized in technical skills that are relevant for organization building no matter what the company does. Don't take switching industries lightly, however—you are moving yourself out of one of your areas of expertise and thereby introducing more risk.

My advice here is fairly brief: look at where the world is going, not where it has been. For example, an enterprise software company would be a more strategic choice than a manufacturer of photographic film. Also think about the skills you have that will be most useful in a new industry. Do you anticipate that there will be an increased need for legal services in a certain industry, let's say environmental lobbying, in the next ten years? Start to move your career in that direction. You want to be in an industry where there is a deficit rather than surplus of people who have your technical skills. Sometimes this is a matter of getting into a nascent industry, but at other times technology or the macroclimate will open up new opportunities in existing industries. This is why it is important to keep up with developments not only in your industry but in the wider economy.

My last piece of advice is that, when you make a jump as big as switching industries, you don't want to also change your functional area. For example, if you are a lawyer in the oil and gas industry, you could make a switch like becoming chief counsel for a technology company. You don't want to go from being a lawyer for an oil company to being a marketing manager for a technology company. The reverse is also true. If you would like to switch your functional area, don't switch your industry as well. In this case, you can go from being a lawyer in the oil and gas industry to being a marketing manager also in the oil and gas industry. Retain at least one of your areas of expertise, even if you want to eventually switch to a different industry or functional area once you are up to speed. Just don't do both at once. Embracing risk is good, but totally knocking out your ability to add value and starting from ground zero is foolish.

Starting a Business

As I shared earlier, I started my own business while doing my MBA and as I was raising a young family. I had already established a successful career in corporate HR, but I had always been drawn to entrepreneurship and wanted to be able to advise a broad range of companies on creating great workplaces. I was energized, prepared, and very ambitious. So I dropped everything I had going and plunged into my new consulting practice full steam. Has it worked for me? Yes. Would I recommend that others start a business this way? The answer is a resounding *no*.

Why? Because businesses take a long time to start. I am not just talking about the paperwork it takes to set up an LLC or the systems you have to put in place in order to be able to process payments or do your business taxes. The biggest reason to give yourself time before you start a business is that it generally takes more than one iteration of a business to figure out what its value proposition is. Unless your business is capital intensive, you should be able to feel out an idea without initially investing a lot of money. So don't quit your day job. Take things one step at a time. Prove the concept before you go all in. This will give you the confidence to know you aren't going to fail once you commit yourself to your new endeavor full time. Starting a business is risky enough that you want to find ways to mitigate the risk you are creating.

There are lots of great books about founding a technology start-up or consultancy, and exploring that journey is beyond the scope of this book. All I can say is that the risk here should be well measured. Most people believe that founding a company means quitting your job altogether and plugging your life's savings into your fledgling company, scrounging money from your family and friends as well (don't do this). This approach might work when you are twenty-two and have little to lose, but it isn't a realistic approach for most of us. Beyond allowing you to continue having money in the bank, small tests prove that your business idea works, and this is the best way to build confidence going forward. That confidence has a business value as you present a proven track record to potential clients.

Putting It All Together

Reading this chapter, you may have noticed that embracing risk in your career doesn't look like what you might have thought. We associate the word "risk" with bungee jumpers, dirt bike riders, and kids who put all of their parents' savings into their social networking app. That is one concept of risk, but it's not one most of us find very tolerable.

Risk doesn't always mean "high risk." Making risky moves has business value if you proceed strategically (the greater the risk, the greater the reward). I believe risk needs to be well considered in order to be effective. That is why this chapter is named *"Taking Action* and Risks," not just "Taking

Risks." You don't want to create instability just because you were told to take more chances; there is no business value there. Introduce risk as it will reward your career. Push yourself out of your comfort zone, but never into anything you are sure you can't succeed at. Challenge yourself, but don't set yourself up to fail. Incorporating risk isn't about making leaps of blind faith, it is about reframing your thinking so that you understand the cost of *not* trying for a project, position, new job, or fledgling company that you have your sights set on.

CHAPTER 9

The Value of Failure and Resilience

The idea that failure is an integral part of one's professional journey is not new. We talk about embracing failure, learning from failure, celebrating failure—all kinds of positive verbs are associated with the idea of things not working out. We have the right idea, but it's just that—an idea. However much we talk about the value of failure, we behave very differently in practice.

If you think about it, we are taught in school from a young age to avoid mistakes—aka failure on a small scale. When you miss points on a math quiz or fail your literature test you aren't celebrated and no one tells you it's an inevitable part of your academic journey. They tell you to study harder and do better. The trend continues in extracurricular activities (no one ever got celebrated for missing a goal, unless you count childhood sports where everyone gets a medal), secondary school, and finally the workplace. We admire the kids who have gotten perfect grades, gained admission to the best universities, attained stellar grades there, and then gone on to the most selective companies or graduate schools. Nothing about this linear and high-achieving path prepares us for messing up.

In my experience, smart people are very uncomfortable with failure for a simple reason: they haven't seen very much of it. It's like we hear the chatter about the inevitability of failure but consider ourselves the exception to this universal truth. When we try something and it doesn't work out, whether it is auditioning for a play and not getting cast or applying for a job and not getting an offer, we take it very hard. Given our conditioning and also our high internal expectations, these reactions aren't surprising. You would not have applied in the first place if you hadn't thought yourself worthy.

In our professional cultures we have myths around success that make failure even less tolerable. On one hand, we perpetuate the myth of the overnight success. Building an app and selling it for millions of dollars sounds easy; nowhere do we see the years of technical training or failed attempts by the company founders that led to their ultimate success. We focus on the IPO, not on the collective thousands of hours of toil it took to get there—or the additional work that will follow now that the company is public. This feeds another idea of ours regarding success. As writer Alain de Botton explains in his TED Talk on reimagining success: the chances now of becoming as wealthy as Bill Gates are as small as the chances of joining the French aristocracy were in the seventeenth century—but that's not how it feels.[1] With a little knowledge of programming, we think we should be as successful as the founders of Google, Facebook, or Instagram. Our collective idea of success has been inflated to an unrealistically high standard because it seems like we *should* be able to create the next industry-disrupting start-up. That was how the others did it, right? What's stopping us? But if such hypersuccess was easy in practice we'd have far more tech billionaires than we do now.

Recalling the very first chapter of this book, feeling entitled to hypersuccess is why it is important to have a well-developed and realistic vision of success. It's not that you can't be as successful as Larry Page or Oprah, but making that your only standard for success is dangerous. If you set crazily high standards for yourself, any amount of failure feels devastating because it moves you further away from an already lofty goal. Remember, this book is all about being personally accountable for your professional success. I want you to pursue your big dreams. Those dreams could involve lots of zeros after the dollar sign. But success doesn't happen overnight and it doesn't *have* to equate to you being a billionaire. Having a well-developed idea of what success means to you at each juncture in your career puts failure in perspective. It helps remind us that failure is one part of a personal journey to a goal you have conviction you can reach. If success to you only means a multibillion-dollar personal net worth, you will take any failure very hard.

This chapter will help you reframe the way you think about failure, explaining why failure is not only an inevitable but also a fundamental part of your career. We will talk about the personal strengths you can cultivate to help you cope with failure, including learning when to push the "Eject" button yourself and call it quits. We will talk about what to do when you have failed. By the conclusion of this chapter, you'll look at failure as less horrifying and more useful in your career than most of us feel it to be.

Why Failure Is Important

We have established that the dirty secret of failure is that, no matter how much we talk about its importance, we all hate it and don't expect it to happen to us. You might have even watched one of those inspirational speeches about embracing failure and either written it off as touchy-feely or loved it—right until you failed at something and remembered that failure sucks.

There is no way around it: failure is painful. But I am here to tell you that failing is okay. Remember, I have coached tens of thousands of people in their journeys, so I have seen a lot of failure. I have seen projects fail, people fail, and companies fail. At times I have seen whole industries fail. Sometimes the events leading up to the catastrophe are outside everyone's control, while other times the disaster is self-initiated. But failure is not the key issue here; the key issue is how you deal with having failed.

The key to making failure constructive is also the reason failure is important: it is an opportunity for growth. People learn the most when they fail or face major setbacks. When you are successful and things are going great, you might be building skills but you are not learning fundamental truths about yourself. I believe people make the least progress when they are doing well. They fall into habits and coast along at a linear rate of growth (and often a low one). Failure—done right—propels you into exponential growth. You are forced to take a hard look at yourself and your business and understand your key flaws. Failure necessitates a total reassessment that does not gloss over the bad bits. When else do we get this opportunity?

I know from experience that failure can lead to progress, but there is scientific data to back up my experiences. Most notably, Carol Dweck, a psychologist from Stanford University, wrote a wonderful book called *Mindset*. The premise of the book is very simple. Relying on our natural abilities like our intelligence or talents to get ahead is misguided (this is tough, Dweck says, because we tend to reward and promote people based on their "brains and talent"). This is called a "fixed mindset." The only way to succeed is to have a "growth mindset": in a growth mindset, we believe in our capacity for hard work and our ability to learn. Her data is supported by the work of Angela Lee Duckworth. Duckworth found in surveys across industries that the best predictor of success is not intelligence, but what she calls "grit," or the ability to keep trying.[2]

Failure, then, is important because it is an opportunity for growth. If you believe this and are willing to work through the failure, then you are in a growth mindset. If your natural abilities fail you, you know it is not the end of the world because hard work and resilience will let you fight another day. You believe you can improve just by applying yourself. Failure means you have a chance to reflect, get better, and recharge. Never let a good crisis go to waste: this is a common quote, but I heard it first when doing YPO (Young Presidents Organization) board work at McKinsey during the financial downturn and it still rings true.[3] Companies and people who have survived a major crisis learn to course correct, pivot, cut costs, find new revenue streams, and, most importantly, establish a better way to achieve their desired outcomes with constrained resources. For many business leaders, surviving a challenging time and coming out on the other side is a rite of passage.

How to Prepare for Failure

We have already established that, while we pay lip service to failure in our culture, as individuals we don't always deal with it gracefully (I would even say that the more successful you are, the more failure hurts). But if you are strategic about it, you can become better acclimated and just better at dealing with failure over time. Getting over that first hump—the first time you really fail at something—is key. Your first failure might not be the most painful one you will ever experience, but it will be the most shocking.

When people do experience failure for the first time, they are generally surprised by it. The high-powered analyst who can't grasp why she is not being promoted and the Harvard MBA manager who just can't get his team motivated don't understand that they are in a place of growth. I am not saying they should embrace being bad at things, but generally they're so stuck on the fact that they *are* bad at something that they can't focus on anything else. They aren't able to move on to the next steps: picking themselves up, figuring out what they learned from the mess, and using that to make something better of themselves.

This sounds strange in theory but works well in practice: you have to prepare to fail. The first step in preparing to fail is recognizing the universal truth of the inevitability of failure. No matter how special you are or how much great planning you do, you will fail. So plan for it. I understand I am promoting a weird cognitive dissonance. On one hand, you're in control of your career and should be confident in your ability to make yourself successful. On the other hand, you have to consider that you might fail. The nuance is that, while you should be assured of your abilities, you have to remember that there are forces beyond your control that can derail your plans. Or sometimes you make a bad choice that's on you—and then you've gone about blowing up your hard work. The point is, it's okay; you just have to be ready to deal with the fallout.

If you can buy into this mindset, the rest is just critical thinking. Remember those decision trees you built in school? If A happens, that could lead to B or C, and if B is the result, then…and so on. When you make a professional decision with any amount of risk, build one of these trees. You want to have a clear idea of all the outcomes of your choice. If plan A doesn't come to fruition, what is your plan B? I know that some people, entrepreneurs especially, say they never considered plan B because they were either so confident in their success or didn't want to acknowledge that failure was a potential outcome. This isn't confidence, it's bad planning. You never want to be blindsided by failure. Understanding the worst-case scenario can help you mitigate some of the damage. It can also help you get started on your recovery plan faster. Failure is always easier to handle when you have thought through all the possible outcomes.

Slowly building a tolerance to failure uses the same logic as the slow-growth skill-building exercises we used for confidence and risk. The advice here changes a little. You build confidence by experiencing small successes and failures; you build risk tolerance by taking small-scale risks. You don't want to practice failure by intentionally pushing yourself to make mistakes, clearly. But testing your ability to map out and be comfortable with your worst-case scenario is a good way to accustom yourself to the idea that things don't always work out. Do a quick temperature test on your level of "disaster preparedness." What would happen if you didn't get a raise this year? What if the product you are working on doesn't launch on time? Looking at an extreme, what would happen if you lost your job tomorrow? These are scary questions to ask. Don't obsess—positivity is important—but have an answer in place.

Finally, if you are going to fail, fail quickly. This advice is ubiquitous in the fast-moving world of Silicon Valley (think of Facebook's "Move fast and break stuff" motto). The way you fail quickly is by constantly evaluating your performance and being willing to call it quits when you have tried everything reasonable and are not getting the results you want.

When Do You Declare Failure?

Most of the experiences I have referenced as hypothetical examples of failure have been situations in which the dropping of the axe was initiated by a manager (you didn't get hired or you got fired). These situations are painful because you have no control, but being the one who decides to call it quits can be equally painful.

Perhaps your struggle is with a project you are heading that isn't working out, a job that's not going well, or even a company you founded that isn't and won't be profitable. Deciding when the time and money invested is no longer worth the return is a hard call to make. We are taught not to be quitters. Sometimes it *is* easier to be let go than to decide for yourself that you have had enough. We have talked about the importance of commitment, but you should never be committed to failure. If failure is going to be the outcome, take action instead of riding out the slow death of your job or company. The trick is having the confidence and perspective to know when to walk away and when to double down.

Quitting a job seems to be the most universal experience of "failure" I come across. Ironically, I don't consider quitting to be a mistake, necessarily; rather, the mistake is taking too long to reach that decision. Perhaps people take so long because they are afraid of looking like a failure or they want to be a star, even though the environment is not set up so they can win. I am going to briefly echo the advice I gave about taking risks in job transitions: if you have received consistently mediocre performance reviews, it is time to start looking for new work. It is very hard to alter a first impression. If your manager has decided you are average, no matter how great your work is, don't hang in there hoping he will wake up one day and decide you are great.

I understand this is a difficult decision to make. When you get a review that declares you average or below average, you will want to prove that review wrong—it's human nature. You should always examine the review to see what is true or useful, but just because your boss or peers said something doesn't mean the assessment is accurate. People will always overestimate their own value and underestimate that of their peers. Small actions can inform a broad-reaching bias. Maybe you made a small clerical error the morning your manager filled out your annual review and it left a bad taste in her mouth. My point is that a performance review offers a very subjective measure of your achievement. You need to decide for yourself whether the review is accurate—and take action from there.

Even if you *are* underperforming, that doesn't necessarily mean you should stay in your job and try to change everyone's minds. It could be that your manager or the position is not the right fit for you. Understand this, so when you look for new work you can articulate why you left. Again, just be careful about staying at your job and deciding you are on a mission to prove your manager wrong. Instead of shoring up your weaknesses, leverage your strengths. The energy you will expend fighting an uphill battle at your current job can be much better spent networking and looking for work in an environment where you will succeed.

When you do decide it's time to go, you need to leave mentally before you leave physically. Keep your day job and devote any time outside of work to your job search. It is perfectly acceptable to get your ducks in a row before quitting. Remember, you have your decision tree—what is plan B? Plan B might even be better than plan A, you just have to take the time to think it through. It is also better to quit than be fired. So decide which feels more like failure to you: (1) giving up on a job and getting a better position elsewhere, (2) getting mediocre reviews and spending years at the same level trying to make everyone believe you are a star, or (3) getting mediocre reviews and eventually getting fired.

Remember my advice earlier about starting a company? Start slowly so you can test ideas and work out your assumed risk—don't quit your day job. The same goes here. It is always easier to find a job when you are employed. The exception is if you feel like you are being abused or pressured to engage in illegal or unethical behavior. Then you should leave no matter what. Potential employers will understand the situation and appreciate your integrity.

Is It a "No" or a "Hard No"?

I find it interesting that the mistake I see people make most frequently is refusing to give up on a bad professional situation (refusing to admit failure). There are some circumstances, though, where the reverse is true; people give in too early. What I see most often is that people do not know the difference between a "soft no," which indicates some room for negotiating, and a "hard no," which indicates a door has been closed.

This is a tricky one. If you push a hard no, you are going to get people upset. But if you don't come back at a soft no, you are going to miss out on some great opportunities. For example, if you are turned down for a job you have applied for, this is a hard no. Trying tactics like going over the hiring manager's head or making your case again will only engender bad feelings. You can, however, go back to the hiring manager and ask for feedback on what would make you a better candidate. Recognize the hard no, but understand where you can still learn from the experience. There are many people I know who have had great careers at organizations that took years to hire them. They were persistent about staying in touch, followed the advice of hiring managers, and were eventually brought on because those same managers recognized that the candidate's passion, tenacity, and willingness to grow are positive traits in employees.

The soft no comes most often when people are building personal connections or trying to win work (submitting proposals, etc.). Again, tread carefully. If you ask a potential mentor or client to a working lunch and she declines, respect the answer, but you could float an offer of coffee or a quick phone call at a later date. Too many people give up at the first sign of hesitation. Selling yourself requires being a little pushy in a very charming way. You have to read the situation and know where the limits are. Unfortunately, this is not something that can be taught, but comes with plenty of socialization and practice.

A great example of the soft no is being wait-listed for undergraduate or graduate programs. Deferral can feel like failure because it is not outright admission—and many people respond to it that way. They accept the deferral and move on, crossing their fingers and hoping they will be accepted in the next round. But this is a soft no, which means there is room for negotiation. Launch a strong but polite campaign for your acceptance. You can send further credentials, ask any connections you have to the university to write letters on your behalf, or even keep up a friendly correspondence with the admissions officers so they know you are very interested. Schools want to admit people who will accept their offer (it helps their rankings), so if you get deferred, go for it. The soft no means it is not the end of the line, you just need to be resilient and creative to win.

Moving on from Failure

Having a plan in place and being able to stomach a hard no is important, but what happens when you actually fail? Your plan will help the transition go more smoothly, but nothing makes getting fired or losing a project feel like a good experience. There are fun learning experiences and then there are ones that are just painful. Failure is a growth opportunity, but that doesn't mean you have to be excited about it.

Failing feels terrible. Having a sense of perspective is important, so you know the difference between a hiccup and a catastrophe, but neither is pleasant. Acknowledging the pain is an important part of moving on from failure, which is why I believe in what I call "structured wallowing." When it comes to your pity party, give yourself a timeline. How long are you going to spend feeling sorry for yourself? Two days? Three? Decide what you need, and then go for it. Cry about your lost job, indulge in your favorite snacks, get beers with your closest friends, go for a ten-mile run (just me?)—whatever it takes for you to recognize and feel the bad parts of failure. And then move on. Assigning a timeline for grieving professional setbacks is important, because eventually you do need to find another job or get to work on another project. Emotions at work have different parameters than emotions in your personal life.

An emotional quality that is important to cultivate as you learn to face failure is self-forgiveness. I knew this term but had never used it in a business context until I stumbled across it in an excellent *Forbes* article.[4] The expert described using self-forgiveness to assess your professional choices without passing judgment on yourself. It is one thing to recognize your mistakes and learn something from failure; it is another to constantly harangue yourself for your bad judgment. This is why the allotted period of wallowing is important. Get it all over and done with at once—and then allow yourself to move on. You want the little voice in your head that inspires self-reflection and asks questions, but you don't want the voice that criticizes your every move. You are accountable for your own success, but you can cut yourself a break. Being overly critical will hold you back. Failure is part of the journey: you are not entitled to success, you have to cultivate it.

Your self-forgiveness will help build your resilience, your ability to put failure in perspective and move on. There aren't any rules for coming back from failure other than it is important to try again—quickly. Just like you have to get back on the bike if you've fallen off, if you get fired you have to get back at the job search. And if you get rejected for one job you have to keep applying for others. The bike becomes scarier the longer you wait to ride it again. The job hunt becomes harder the longer you let applications linger and e-mails go unanswered. This behavior was proven on a large scale during the 2008–09 economic downturn. The unemployment rate fell at times, but it wasn't because people had gotten jobs. They had just gotten discouraged looking and given up altogether.[5] With failure often comes a sense of inertia associated with a loss of confidence. This is why confidence and resilience are so important; when things don't work out you need to believe it is worth it to try again.

One of my favorite recent stories of resilience is that of Brian Acton, a founder of the messaging app WhatsApp. In 2009 he applied for a job at Facebook and was rejected.[6] Instead of deciding he was going to give up working in tech and admit defeat, he went on to found his own company. Which was then acquired by—you guessed it—Facebook in 2014 for $19 billion, probably a bit more than his Facebook compensation for those five years had he been hired.[7]

Putting It All Together

Talking about failure without sounding like a harbinger of gloom and doom is difficult. No matter the positive cultural conversation we have cultivated, our personal feelings about failure are usually anything but encouraging. It is difficult to be 100 percent committed to taking control of your career knowing that you are accepting responsibility for the failures you will encounter along the way. But you will fail many times in your journey. After allowing yourself a brief interlude of despair, switch into your growth mindset and recognize that this is a moment for you to learn. Upward and onward.

A final thought about failure: in a widely watched TED Talk, Elizabeth Gilbert, author of the blockbuster seller *Eat, Pray, Love,* describes her early years trying to make it as a struggling writer.[8] For years and years she submitted essays and manuscripts to editors only to be rejected. So why did she keep trying? In other words, what fed her resilience, and ultimately led to great success? In Gilbert's case, she loved writing more than she hated failure. Approach your professional journey with the same passion. Be more committed to your dreams than you are intimidated by the idea of failing. This kind of conviction can make a bad presentation or botched interview feel small compared with the faith you have in your greater ambitions.

Conclusion

My hope is that you finished the last chapter and realized how much control you have over your own professional success. You now know your goals, how to make the best of your continuing education, how to plan your time, how to build your own brand, how to acquire the skills you need at work, how to use external support, how to deliver on your commitments, how to take risks, how to deal with failure: everything you need to win big in your career. In essence, you have the power to be your own talent agent, manager, and PR person.

My final advice for you is to be bold. Envision your success and buy into that dream with conviction. With the tools described in this book, you will know what to do if it all goes to pieces. Fail fast and pick up the pieces even faster, knowing that this is just part of the journey. You have to take big risks to achieve your biggest dreams.

In your journey, make sure to keeping looking for your genius. You have the potential to do something amazing—change the world, break the glass ceiling in your industry, or live a life aligned with your values, spending time on the things you really care about. This genius doesn't rest with a mentor or anyone else; it is your job to find it and use it to make the most of your career.

Keeping track of people's professional journeys is my full-time job because helping people hit their goals and develop into incredible leaders is my passion. To that end, please e-mail me at debby@thementormyth.com to share your own goals and what you are doing to achieve them. Remember—it's boring to be average so go ahead and light the world on fire.

NOTES

Introduction

1. Bert Gervais, "10 Killer Questions to Make the Most of Your Mentor Meeting," *Forbes,* online edition, February 28, 2014, accessed May 21, 2015, http://www.forbes.com/sites/theyec/2014/02/28/10-killer-questions-to-make-the-most-of-your-mentor-meeting/.
2. Young Entrepreneur Council, "12 Questions You Should Ask Your Mentor ASAP," *Inc.* magazine, online edition, July 16, 2014, accessed May 21, 2015, http://www.inc.com/young-entrepreneur-council/the-12-questions-you-should-be-asking-your-mentor.html.
3. "January—National Mentoring Month," 2015 National Mentoring Month Campaign, accessed May 21, 2015, http://www.nationalmentoringmonth.org/.
4. Robert I. Sutton, "Five Signs That Your Mentor Is Giving You Bad Advice," *Harvard Business Review,* online edition, December 11, 2013, accessed April 27, 2015, https://hbr.org/2013/12/five-signs-that-your-mentor-is-giving-you-bad-advice/.
5. Carolyn O'Hara, "How to Break Up with Your Mentor," *Harvard Business Review,* online edition, May 29, 2014, accessed April 27, 2015, https://hbr.org/2014/05/how-to-break-up-with-your-mentor.

Chapter 1

1. David Sadker and Karen R. Zittleman, *Still Failing at Fairness: How Gender Bias Cheats Girls and Boys in School and What We Can Do About it,* New York: Simon and Schuster, 2009, 24.
2. Neil Howe and William Strauss, *Millennials Rising,* New York: Vintage, 2000, 4.

3. Jeanne Meister, "Job Hopping Is the 'New Normal' for Millennials: Ways to Prevent a Human Resource Nightmare," Forbes, August 1, 2014, accessed August 1, 2015, [http://www.forbes.com/sites/jeannemeister/2012/08/14/job-hopping-is-the-new-normal-for-millennials-three-ways-to-prevent-a-human-resource-nightmare/.

4. Shawn Achor, *The Happiness Advantage* (New York: Crown Business, 2010), 44.

5. Lawrence Mishel and Alyssa Davies, "CEO Pay Continues to Rise as Typical Workers Are Paid Less," Economic Policy Institute, January 5, 2015, accessed January 5, 2015, http://www.epi.org/publication/ceo-pay-continues-to-rise/.

Chapter 2

1. Marlisse Silver Sweeney, "The Female Lawyer Exodus," Women in the World, *The Daily Beast*, updated July 13, 2013, accessed August 1, 2014, http://www.thedailybeast.com/witw/articles/2013/07/31/the-exodus-of-female-lawyers.html.

2. Janelle Jones and John Schmitt, "A College Degree Is No Guarantee," Center for Economic Policy Research, May 2014, accessed August 1, 2014, http://www.cepr.net/documents/black-coll-grads-2014-05.pdf.

3. Richard Vedder, Christopher Denhart, and Jonathan Robe, "Why Are Recent College Graduates Underemployed?" The Center for College Affordability & Productivity, January 28, 2013, accessed August 1, 2014, http://centerforcollegeaffordability.org/research/studies/underemployment-of-college-graduates/.

4. "Annual Report of the CFPB Student Loan Ombudsman," Consumer Financial Protection Bureau, October 16, 2012, accessed August 1, 2014, http://files.consumerfinance.gov/f/201210_cfpb_Student-Loan-Ombudsman-Annual-Report.pdf.

5. "College Admits Class of '18," *Harvard Gazette,* March 27, 2014, accessed August 1, 2014, http://news.harvard.edu/gazette/story/2014/03/college-admits-class-of-18/.

6. Sandra Stalkis and Paul Skomsvold, "New Graduates at Work," Stats in Brief: U.S. Department of Education, March 2014, accessed August 1, 2014, http://nces.ed.gov/pubs2014/2014003.pdf.

7. "Average Student Debt Climbing: $29,400 for Class of 2012," Institute for College Access & Success, December 4, 2013, accessed

August 1, 2014, http://www.ticas.org/files/pub/Student_Debt _and_the_Class_of_2012_NR.pdf.

8. "Employment Projections," Bureau of Labor Statistics, last updated April 2, 2015, accessed August 1, 2014, http://www.bls.gov/emp/ ep_chart_001.htm.

9. "Occupational Employment, Job Openings, and Worker Characteristics," Employment Projections, Bureau of Labor Statistics, last updated December 19, 2013, accessed August 1, 2014, http:// www.bls.gov/emp/ep_table_107.htm.

10. Meg Jay, "Why 30 Is Not the New 20," TED Talk, February 2013, http://www.ted.com/talks/meg_jay_why_30_is_not_the_new_20.

11. Orit Gadiesh and Julie Coffman, "Survey: Why Don't More Women Rise to the Top?" HBR Blog Network, updated January 7, 2010, accessed August 1, 2014, http://blogs.hbr.org/2010/01/ survey-why-dont-more-women-rise/.

Chapter 3

1. Brigid Schulte, *Overwhelmed: Work, Love, and Play When No One Has Time*, New York: Sarah Crichton Books, 2014, Chapter 3. Kindle edition.

2. Tina Fey, "Confessions of a Juggler," *New Yorker,* February 14, 2011, accessed August 1, 2014, http://www.newyorker.com/magazine/ 2011/02/14/confessions-of-a-juggler.

3. Brian Tracy, "Plan Ahead and Increase Productivity," *Brian Tracy International,* accessed August 1, 2014, http://www.briantracy.com/ blog/time-management/plan-ahead-and-increase-productivity/.

4. Brigid Schulte, The Test of Time: A Busy Working Mother Tries to Figure Out Where All Her Time Is Going," *Washington Post,* January 17, 2010, accessed August 15, 2014, http://www.washingtonpost .com/wp-dyn/content/article/2010/01/11/AR2010011101999.html.

5. Marybeth J. Mattingly and Suzanne M. Bianci, "Gender Differences in the Quantity and Quality of Free Time: The U.S. Experience," Social Forces 81.3 (2003):1022–1024.

6. Ellen Galinsky, Kerstin Aumann, and James T. Bond, "Time Ares Changing," Families and Work Institute: 2008 National Study of the Changing Workforce (Revised 2011).

7. Brigid Schulte, *Overwhelmed: Work, Love, and Play When No One Has Time,* New York: Sarah Crichton Books, 2014, Chapter 2. Kindle edition.

8. Jennifer Aaker, "Rethinking Time: The Power of Multipliers," Lean In, accessed August 15, 2014. http://leanin.org/education/rethinking-time-the-power-of-multipliers/.

9. Agata Baszczak-Boxe, "The Secrets of Short Sleepers: How Do They Thrive on Less Sleep?" CBS News, June 27, 2014, accessed August 15, 2014, http://www.cbsnews.com/news/the-secrets-of-short-sleepers-how-do-they-thrive-on-less-sleep/

10. Sam Fahmy, "Regular Exercise Better Than Stimulants at Reducing Fatigue," *University of Georgia Research Magazine*, Winter 2007, accessed September 11, 2015, http://researchmagazine.uga.edu/winter2007/printregularexercise.htm,

11. Randy Pausch, "Time Management," Carnegie Mellon University, accessed August 15, 2014, http://www.cs.virginia.edu/~robins/TimeManagementTalk.html.

12. Stephen Covey, *First Things First,* Miami: Mango Media, Inc., 2015, The Urgency Addiction: Importance. Kindle edition.

Chapter 4

1. Janie Kliever, "Why We Respond Emotionally to Numbers," *Canva* blog, April 16, 2015, accessed June 25, 2015, https://designschool.canva.com/blog/design-number/.

2. James Wood, "New MLA Deborah Drever Suspended from NDP Caucus Over 'Homophobic' Remark Under Photo," *Calgary Herald*, May 22, 2015, accessed June 25, 2015, http://calgaryherald.com/news/politics/new-mla-deborah-drever-suspended-from-ndp-caucus-over-homophobic-remark-under-photo.

Chapter 5

1. "10 Ways to Be Good," The School of Life, accessed June 25, http://www.theschooloflife.com/london/business/case-studies/virtues-project/.

2. Tomas Chamorro-Premuzic, "Why Do So Many Incompetent Men Become Leaders?" *Harvard Business Review,* August 22, 2013, accessed June 25, 2015, https://hbr.org/2013/08/why-do-so-many-incompetent-men/.

3. Hayley Peterson, "8 Outrageous Remarks By Lululemon Founder Chip Wilson," *Business Insider,* December 10, 2013, accessed June 25, 2015, http://www.businessinsider.com/outrageous-remarks-by-lululemon-founder-chip-wilson-2013-12.

4. Erin Reid and Sarah Green, "Why We Pretend to be Workaholics," *Harvard Business Review*, May 7, 2015, accessed June 25, 2014, https://hbr.org/2015/05/why-we-pretend-to-be-workaholics.
5. Madeline Stone, "Marissa Mayer Sent 18 Yahoo Employees on a Free Trip to Hawaii," *Business Insider*, April 14, 2015, accessed June 25, 2014, http://www.businessinsider.com/marissa-mayer-sent-yahoo-employees-to-hawaii-2015-4.
6. Rob Asghar, "Incompetence Rains, Er, Reigns: What the Peter Principle Means Today," *Forbes*, August 14, 2014, accessed June 25, 2015, http://www.forbes.com/sites/robasghar/2014/08/14/incompetence-rains-er-reigns-what-the-peter-principle-means-today/.

Chapter 6

1. Herminia Ibarra, Nancy M. Carter, and Christine Silva, "Why Men Still Get More Promotions Than Women," *Harvard Business Review*, September 2010, accessed June 25, 2015, https://hbr.org/2010/09/why-men-still-get-more-promotions-than-women.
2. Allie Kline, "Why This AOL Executive Chooses Her Mentors—Wisely," *Fortune*, April 29, 2015, accessed June 25, 2015, http://fortune.com/2015/04/29/allie-kline-importance-of-mentors/.
3. Sheryl Sandberg, *Lean In* (New York: Knopf, 2013), 70-71.
4. Dan Schawbel, "Margaret Keane: How Synchrony Financial Built A Winning Culture," *Forbes*, May 10, 2015, accessed June 25, 2015, http://www.forbes.com/sites/danschawbel/2015/05/10/margaret-keane-how-synchrony-financial-built-a-winning-culture/.
5. Sylvia Ann Hewlett, "The Real Benefit of Finding a Sponsor," *Harvard Business Review*, January 26, 2011, accessed June 25, 2015, https://hbr.org/2011/01/the-real-benefit-of-finding-a/.
6. Sylvia Ann Hewlett "The Right Way to Find a Career Sponsor," *Harvard Business Review*, September 11, 2013, accessed June 25, 2015, https://hbr.org/2013/09/the-right-way-to-find-a-career-sponsor/.
7. Sylvia Ann Hewlett "The Real Benefit of Finding a Sponsor," *Harvard Business Review*, January 26, 2011, accessed June 25, 2015, https://hbr.org/2011/01/the-real-benefit-of-finding-a/.

Chapter 7

1. Mathew Ingram, "Lessons in How to Go Viral: Use the 'Bored at Work' Network," Gigaom Research, August 13, 2010, accessed

June 25, 2015, https://gigaom.com/2010/08/13/lessons-in-how -to-go-viral-use-the-bored-at-work-network/.

Chapter 8

1. Rebecca Rifkin, "Average U.S. Retirement Age Rises to 62," Gallup, April 28, 2014, accessed June 25, 2015, http://www.gallup .com/poll/168707/average-retirement-age-rises.aspx;

2. Gary Strauss, "2015 Raises Expected to Be 3% Next Year," USA Today, September 8, 2014, accessed June 25, 2015, http://www .usatoday.com/story/money/business/2014/09/07/2015-pay -raises-should-average-3/15136423/.

3. Justin Brady, "The Troubling flaws in How We Select Experts," *Washington Post*, June 25, 2014, accessed June 25, 2015, http:// www.washingtonpost.com/blogs/innovations/wp/2014/06/25/ the-troubling-flaws-in-how-we-select-experts/.

4. Cameron Keng, "Employees Who Stay in Companies Longer Than Two Years Get Paid 50% Less," *Forbes*, June 22, 2014, accessed September 15, 2015, http://www.forbes.com/sites/cameronkeng/ 2014/06/22/employees-that-stay-in-companies-longer-than -2-years-get-paid-50-less/.

Chapter 9

1. Alain De Botton, "A Kinder, Gentler Philosophy of Success," TED Talk, July 2009, accessed June 25, 2015, http://www.ted .com/talks/alain_de_botton_a_kinder_gentler_philosophy_of _success?language=en.

2. Angela Lee Duckworth, "The Key to Success? Grit," TED Talk, April 2013, accessed June 25, 2015, http://www.ted.com/talks/ angela_lee_duckworth_the_key_to_success_grit?language=en.

3. Mlladen Fruk, Stephen Hall, and Devesh Mittal, "Never Let a Good Crisis Go to Waste," *McKinsey Quarterly*, October 2013, accessed June 25, 2015, http://www.mckinsey.com/insights/ strategy/never_let_a_good_crisis_go_to_waste.

4. Denise Restauri, "Top 10 Traits of Self-Made Women: How Many Do You Have?" *Forbes*, June 11, 2015, accessed June 25, 2015, http://www.forbes.com/sites/deniserestauri/2015/06/11/top -10-traits-of-self-made-women-how-many-do-you-have/.

5. Yuki Noguchi, "Discouraged in Hunt for a Job, Many Stop Looking," NPR, September 14, 2012, accessed June 25, 2015, http://

www.npr.org/2012/09/14/161095920/discouraged-in-hunt-for-a
-job-many-stop-looking.

6. Julie Bort, "Facebook Rejected WhatsApp Co-Founder Brian Action for a Job Back in 2009," *Business Insider,* February 19, 2014, accessed June 25, 2015, http://www.businessinsider.com/facebook-rejected-whatsapp-co-founder-brian-acton-for-a-job-back-in-2009-2014-2.

7. Parmy Olson, "Facebook Closes $19 Billion WhatsApp Deal," *Forbes,* October 6, 2014, accessed June 25, 2015, http://www.forbes.com/sites/parmyolson/2014/10/06/facebook-closes-19-billion-whatsapp-deal/.

8. Elizabeth Gilbert,"Success, Failure, and the Drive to Keep Creating," TED Talk, April 2014, accessed June 25, 2015, http://www.ted.com/talks/elizabeth_gilbert_success_failure_and_the_drive_to_keep_creating/transcript?language=en.

REFERENCES

Gervais, Bert. "10 Killer Questions to Make the Most of Your Mentor Meeting." *Forbes*, online edition, February 28, 2014. Accessed May 21, 2015. http://www.forbes.com/sites/theyec/2014/02/28/10-killer-questions-to-make-the-most-of-your-mentor-meeting/.

O'Hara, Carolyn. "How to Break Up with Your Mentor." *Harvard Business Review*, online edition, May 29, 2014. Accessed April 27, 2015. https://hbr.org/2014/05/how-to-break-up-with-your-mentor.

Sutton, Robert I. "Five Signs That Your Mentor Is Giving You Bad Advice." *Harvard Business Review*, online edition, December 11, 2013. Accessed April 27, 2015. https://hbr.org/2013/12/five-signs-that-your-mentor-is-giving-you-bad-advice/.

Young Entrepreneur Council. "12 Questions You Should Ask Your Mentor ASAP." *Inc.* magazine, online edition, July 16, 2014. Accessed May 21, 2015. http://www.inc.com/young-entrepreneur-council/the-12-questions-you-should-be-asking-your-mentor.html.

INDEX

ACKNOWLEDGMENTS

I am so thankful to do work that I love and that makes a difference in the lives of so many. This book was a pleasure to write and there are so many people to thank:

Kelsey Grode, thank you for making it all possible and sharing my passion for workplaces and helping people succeed in their careers. *The Mentor Myth* never would have happened without you.

Todd, thank you for being the best partner a wife could ever wish for and for encouraging me on days when felt like I bit off more than I could chew.

Thank you to the entire team at Bibliomotion, Inc. You are such a passionate, professional group that makes the editing, production, designing, promotion, and everything behind the scenes happen seamlessly to launch a great book.

Carly Watters and P.S. Literary Agency, for believing in my ideas through version 1.0, 2.0, 3.0, and beyond.

I am grateful to the members and leadership of the Young Presidents' Organization. You are all such an inspiration and one couldn't ask for a more supportive peer group.

Thank you to my team at Inspired HR. You inspire me

every day with your dedication to building great workplaces for employees everywhere.

To all the mentors, sponsors, peer groups, and clients who have helped me along the way.

Lastly, to my friends and family. Thank you for your support, encouragement, carpooling, and inspiration.

ABOUT THE AUTHOR

Debby Carreau is the Founder and CEO of Inspired HR, a human resources firm serving clients across North America and globally. She is often asked to speak and write about twenty-first century workplace issues and serve as a judge for entrepreneurial competitions. Debby is a sought after public speaker on remote work, the move to contingent workforces, women in the workplace, and the importance of diversity. Debby's recent coverage includes the *Harvard Business Review*, the *Wall Street Journal*, CNBC, *Bloomberg Businessweek*, the *Huffington Post*, MSNBC, the BBC, and many others. Debby has been recognized multiple times as one of Canada's Most Powerful Women™ for her work helping businesses create great workplaces and deliver superior business results by making better decisions about human capital.

Debby Carreau can be reached through either of her websites:
www.inspired-hr.com
or www.debbycarreau.com
and at
www.twitter.com/DebbyCarreau
www.facebook.com/DebbyCarreau

I would love to hear from you, please keep in touch!

 @DebbyCarreau

 Debby Carreau

 https://ca.linkedin.com/in/debbycarreau

 DebbyCarreau

Debby Carreau, MBA, CHRP
The Mentor Myth Keynotes

The Mentor Myth

Mentors are overutilized, undertrained and, as studies show, underdeliver. From an employer's perspective, assigning a mentor is often a quick fix to a larger problem. From an employee's perspective, a lack of formal mentorship is seen as a serious hindrance to a successful career. Learn how to create a culture of personal accountability and take your business to a whole new level of performance.

Bringing your workplace into the twenty-first century

Every day we hear about new workplace trends, but which ones warrant incorporation into your business? As the global economy improves and the war for talent heats up again, top employers are garnering the attention of your employees. Some have created some great Disneyland-like campuses; others offer nap pods, unlimited vacation, and remote work. What will work for you and how do you compete in this talent war?

Optimizing your human capital strategy

Learn how to transition your HR department from a cost center to a strategic weapon. Learn how to leverage your people as your competitive advantage by becoming an employer of choice, reducing bureaucracy, and maximizing productivity.

Redefining talent management through personal accountability, based on *The Mentor Myth*

Based on *The Mentor Myth*, this interactive workshop will provide practical insights on how to rethink your approach to your own career and your organizations' human capital. Most talent management programs are irrelevant to today's business challenges. Budget cuts, shifting demographics, disruptive technologies, and economic uncertainty have changed the playing field and what's required of employees to thrive. Those organizations that have not shifted their talent management strategy are at great economic risk. It is evident that a new normal in business is emerging and this session gives you a framework to drive personal accountability and become your own "talent agent."

To invite Debby to speak please email
media@debbycarreau.com